100+ Exercises to
Boost Your <u>Resilience</u>,
<u>Determination</u>, and <u>Grit!</u>

LEVEL

UP

Your Mental Toughness
BOOT CAMP

MICHELLE RIBEIRO

ADAMS MEDIA
NEW YORK   LONDON   TORONTO   SYDNEY   NEW DELHI

Adams Media
An Imprint of Simon & Schuster, Inc.
57 Littlefield Street
Avon, Massachusetts 02322

First Adams Media trade paperback edition April 2021

ADAMS MEDIA and colophon are trademarks of Simon & Schuster.

For information about special discounts for bulk purchases, please contact Simon & Schuster Special Sales at 1-866-506-1949 or business@simonandschuster.com.

The Simon & Schuster Speakers Bureau can bring authors to your live event. For more information or to book an event contact the Simon & Schuster Speakers Bureau at 1-866-248-3049 or visit our website at www.simonspeakers.com.

Interior design by Erin Alexander and Michelle Kelly

Manufactured in the United States of America

1 2021

Library of Congress Cataloging-in-Publication Data has been applied for.

ISBN 978-1-5072-1544-9
ISBN 978-1-5072-1545-6 (ebook)

DEDICATION

To my family and friends, who have supported me through my darkest moments and who always encourage me to follow my dreams.

And to anyone who struggles with their mental health. You are tougher than you realize. It's not easy to do the work, yet here you are. Thank you for showing up, and may this offering assist you in coming home to yourself.

CONTENTS

Chapter 3

Exercises to Cultivate Emotional Resilience | 57

Chapter 4

Exercises to Build Grit | 81

Chapter 5
Exercises to Maintain Patience and Self-Control | 103

Chapter 6
Exercises to Increase Optimism | 123

Chapter 7
Exercises to Confront Stress | 145

Chapter 8
Exercises to Forge Self-Confidence | 171

Chapter 9

Exercises to Improve Self-Awareness | 191

Chapter 10

Exercises to Embrace Failure | 211

Chapter 11

Exercises to Hone Attentional Focus | 229

INTRODUCTION

Wishing you could bounce back from difficult situations faster? Looking for more confidence in your abilities? Longing to banish self-doubt and finally go after the things you want? You have the capacity to achieve all of this and more—you just need to level up your mental toughness!

Mental toughness is what determines how you respond to the pressures and challenges of life. Whatever comes your way, it enables you to weather the storm and come out on the other side victorious. You may think the amount of mental toughness you have is predetermined, but it's not! It is a skill, and just like every other skill, it can be learned and strengthened—or "leveled up." In the same way you'd improve your physique by hitting the gym and cutting out junk food, developing inner strength requires that you cultivate good practices of mind while eliminating bad practices. You hold the power to renovate your internal landscape.

In *Level Up*, you'll claim that power and cultivate your toughest self. The 120 activities that follow will help you build on your existing level of mental toughness, eliminating any obstacles in your way and tapping into your full, gritty potential. You'll:

- Build your emotional vocabulary
- Make friends with accountability
- Uncover your emotional blind spots
- Design an environment that promotes success
- Hone your impulse control
- And so much more!

But before jumping into these exercises, you'll take a closer look at mental toughness, from the different elements that make up a mentally tough person to the importance of habits and how to create good ones that aid in your success. You'll also discover tips for making the most of each activity that follows, as well as what you may want to have on hand.

Think of this book as your mental boot camp for making your mind stronger and more agile. And remember: The more you commit to these exercises, the greater transformation you will experience. It's time to create lasting change in your life. Get ready to level up!

CHAPTER 1

WHAT IS MENTAL TOUGHNESS?

Mental toughness is defined as the capacity to deal effectively with stressors, pressures, and challenges to perform to the best of your abilities—regardless of the circumstances in which you may find yourself. Possessing this trait means that you are confident in who you are and have the inner strength to face down and rebound from whatever situations are thrown at you. Often the term is used synonymously with *grit* or *resilience*, and though related, they're each distinct concepts. Mental toughness encompasses these concepts—and more.

In this chapter, you will prepare to take your own mental toughness to the next level by first exploring each of these different concepts in more detail. You'll then learn more about why a solid foundation of inner strength is crucial to happiness and success. After assessing your current level of mental toughness, you'll uncover the power of habits and goals in advancing to a higher level. Finally, you'll find tips and suggestions for making the most out of each exercise in this book. So are you ready to become someone who not only survives but thrives? Someone who lives up to their full potential? Let's dive in!

CHARACTERISTICS OF MENTALLY TOUGH PEOPLE

Bethany Hamilton, George Foreman, Lady Gaga, and David Goggins are exemplary models of mental toughness. What do they have in common?

1. **Emotional resiliency:** They know that emotional reactions predicate behavior, and they always try to maintain a balance between emotions and logic. They are in control of their emotions—not the other way around.
2. **Grit:** They are passionate and conscientious about their work and have a strong why behind everything they do. This makes it easier for them to stick to it for the long haul.
3. **Patience and self-control:** They work persistently toward their long-term goals and view success as a marathon, not a sprint. They know that mastery takes time and practice, and they have the self-control to choose progress over distractions and immediate gratification.
4. **Motivation:** They have an unwavering commitment to their goals. They know success takes more than a desire for change—it takes constant practice.
5. **Optimism:** They face fear and discomfort again and again, all while maintaining a positive mindset. They are able to find the silver linings in even the darkest clouds.
6. **Stress management:** They have a strong handle on their stress levels during difficult situations, keeping calm in order to make quick decisions and do what needs to be done.

7. **Confidence:** They are confident in their abilities and don't let self-doubt get in the way of going after what they want.
8. **Self-awareness:** They have a deep understanding of their needs, values, and goals. This understanding is what guides them in their pursuit of success.
9. **The ability to embrace failure:** They don't shy away from calculated risk, because they're not afraid to fail. They see failure as an opportunity for growth.
10. **Attentional focus:** They focus on their goals and priorities, making a continual commitment to what is important to them.

These are the skills that create true inner strength—and every great thing that comes along with it—and they are what you will be building in the exercises later in this book.

Of course, you don't have to look to the world stage to see examples of mental toughness. You need only look around at the people in your life who have been through hardship but continue to persevere and maintain optimism. They trust their ability to bounce back from adversity even stronger than before, and they may even welcome the challenge!

BENEFITS OF BEING MENTALLY TOUGH

So what can you expect to gain from befriending discomfort, putting unconventional effort into your life, or embracing failure? The benefits of toughening up mentally can manifest in many different areas, from your career path to your personal relationships to your health. Main benefits you can expect are self-empowerment, stronger connections with others, enhanced performance in both professional and personal realms, and increased resiliency.

SELF-EMPOWERMENT

By leveling up your mental toughness, you'll nurture an unshakeable belief in your abilities and the confidence needed to shrug off criticism and move beyond your current situation toward the life of your dreams. You'll uncover new perspectives on outdated beliefs that are holding you back from the life you want to live. For example, moving from a self-critical fixed mindset of "I can't change who I am; failure is weakness and should be avoided at all costs" to a self-assured growth mindset of "I am capable and open to learning; mistakes are an essential part of long-term development."

STRONGER CONNECTIONS

The benefits of mental toughness will also manifest in your relationships with others. An outward attitude of positivity, patience, and reliability is always appreciated and often reciprocated. People will be motivated to treat you with the same kindness and respect that you are extending to them. Additionally, the emotion-regulation skills that you build as you increase your mental toughness can improve your communication, helping you to control and better express strong emotions such as anger that often get in the way of effective conversations.

ENHANCED PERFORMANCE

One of the greatest benefits of toughness is the advantage it yields in attaining success. Until recently, research and interest in this area has tended to focus on elite athletes. Nowadays, mental toughness is seen as a key component in achieving peak performance and success in all areas of life. It's become a highly sought-after attribute in business, academic, social, and personal settings. No matter what realm you're looking to improve in, mental toughness will help you to focus in a distracting world, perform under pressure, and face obstacles calmly so that you can get things done—and done well. If you're in a leadership role, whether as an employer, in a club, or on a sports team, mental toughness will equip you with the awareness and drive you need to motivate others and help them achieve their own goals. If you're an entrepreneur, it will encourage you to embrace fear, understanding failure as potential for growth. And if your current idea of success is to be in the best physical shape of your life, enhanced performance will come in the form of greater determination, consistency with workouts, and more.

INCREASED RESILIENCE

Perhaps the greatest benefit of leveling up your mental toughness is the resiliency that is built along with it—the ability to handle the stresses, disappointments, and surprises of daily life more effectively and calmly. Instead of getting stuck on the things that are outside of your control, this inner strength nurtures a focus on what you can control. You bounce back from the unexpected and upsetting more quickly, accepting that there is nothing to be gained from dwelling on what has happened (or what may happen in the future); all you can do is act with intention to learn and grow from the experience.

ASSESSING YOUR MENTAL TOUGHNESS

Now that you have a deeper understanding of mental toughness, it's time to figure out where you currently stand on this scale. Self-reflection is an important aspect of personal development because it provides valuable feedback that you can work with. When was the last time you stopped to reflect on your strengths and weaknesses? On what areas of your life are you thriving, and which could use some improvement?

The aim of assessment is to increase your self-awareness (a key part of mental toughness in itself) and help you determine where you should be concentrating your efforts as you continue through the rest of this chapter and the exercises in this book.

Be honest with yourself, but remain positive. No matter where you currently are on the scale of mental toughness, keep in mind that this is just the beginning of your journey. Greater inner strength is waiting for you around the corner! As psychotherapist and father of the self-esteem movement Nathaniel Branden once said, "The first step toward change is awareness. The second step is acceptance."

SELF-ASSESSMENT

One way you can evaluate your current level of mental toughness is through a self-assessment. To complete this assessment, take some time to answer the following questions. Consider keeping track of your answers in a notebook.

Emotional Resilience:

- How quickly do you bounce back from setbacks and failures?
- Do you have strategies to boost your mood when you're down?

Grit:

- Do you give up quickly, or stick to things no matter what?
- Are you enthusiastic about the tasks you have to do?

Patience and Self-Control:

- Do you have clear boundaries with yourself and with others?
- How do you handle boredom?

Goals and Motivation:

- Do you have a clear vision for your future?
- Are you on track to where you want to be in terms of your personal and professional development?

Optimism:

- Do you tend to focus on the possible negative outcomes or the possible positive outcomes of a situation?
- Is your self-talk generally positive or negative?

Stress:

- Can you keep calm and composed under pressure?
- Do you have strategies for dealing with stressful situations?

Self-Confidence:
* How confident are you in your own abilities?
* Are you able to initiate difficult conversations?

Self-Awareness:
* What are your greatest strengths and weaknesses? Your best and worst habits?
* Do you know how others would answer these questions about you?

Failure:
* Do you feel more motivated or less motivated after experiencing a failure?
* How do you handle rejection?

Attentional Focus:
* Can you focus on what's important and block out all distractions?
* Can you remain in control despite unexpected, uncontrollable events?

If you can answer these questions honestly, you should have a better idea of which chapters you'll want to focus on most to strengthen your mental toughness. Keep in mind that there may be some overlap with these questions, as the themes do connect to one another.

FORMAL ASSESSMENT

For a more formal appraisal of your mental toughness, you can complete assessments online. The most widely recognized and accredited are the MTQ Assessments, developed by Peter Clough and Doug Strycharczyk. Their original assessment, called the MTQ48, was created to meet the needs of senior managers who wanted to understand why some people could handle stressors, pressure, and challenges well while others couldn't, and how to improve this ability. It's a forty-eight-item questionnaire that takes just ten minutes to complete. A few variations of the MTQ48 assessment include MTQLite, MTQ4Cs, and MTQPlus. All are readily available online.

These globally recognized psychometric tools measure what are referred to as "the four Cs" of mental toughness:

1. Control
2. Commitment
3. Challenge
4. Confidence

The four Cs represent your inner strength and outer orientation. Within these, the MTQ assessments measure eight subscales:

1. **Life control:** (Control scale) The extent to which you believe you are in control of your life and circumstances.
2. **Emotional control:** (Control scale) The extent to which you can control your anxieties and emotions, and how likely you are to reveal your emotional states to others.

3. **Goal orientation:** (Commitment scale) The extent to which you are able to effectively set goals and targets.
4. **Achievement orientation:** (Commitment scale) The extent to which you are reliable to deliver on your commitments.
5. **Risk orientation:** (Challenge scale) The extent to which you are open to change and new experiences.
6. **Learning orientation:** (Challenge scale) The extent to which you are likely to view a challenge as an opportunity.
7. **Confidence in abilities:** (Confidence scale) A measure of self-belief; the extent to which you believe you have the ability to perform productively and efficiently.
8. **Interpersonal confidence:** (Confidence scale) The extent to which you have the ability to influence others.

The control and commitment scales together represent the resilience part of the mental toughness definition—the ability to bounce back from setbacks and failures. The challenge and confidence scales together represent the confidence part of the mental toughness definition—the ability to spot and seize an opportunity.

If you decide to take one of these formal assessments, be sure to record your results. Use these results to set your mental toughness goals and pinpoint which exercise chapter(s) you may want to focus on in order to achieve these goals.

USING HABITS TO BUILD MENTAL TOUGHNESS

Being born mentally tough would be ideal, but most people just aren't. For the majority, the way to develop this vital trait lies in habits. If you don't quite understand the science of how habits work, this might be the most important step you take toward leveling up!

Mental toughness is like a muscle—it's built incrementally through daily actions. And habits are the small actions and decisions you make every single day—the behaviors you repeat routinely. These routine behaviors include the thoughts that you think, emotions you experience, words you use, and so on. Most of these habits are so ingrained in your life (because you've done them over and over throughout the years) that they tend to occur subconsciously as a default response. They don't require thought; they just happen naturally.

Habits are said to account for about 40 percent of your behavior each day; that means that almost half the time you're basically living on autopilot! When you're trying to build your mental toughness muscle, autopilot is not an option. It will take deliberate and persistent effort to develop the attributes of mental toughness, and you'll have to alter some of your current patterns of behavior. When you break bad habits, good habits become more effective.

The toughest people—and the most successful people—have good mental habits. They habitually use their time wisely, challenge themselves, and regulate their emotions. They habitually look for silver linings and take calculated risks. They habitually set goals and work hard to achieve their objectives. They are habitual optimists. While it's great to strive for some future target, it's the sum of your daily habits that will ultimately help get you there.

THE HABIT LOOP

The key to both changing bad habits and developing new, good habits is to understand the concept of the habit loop. This psychological pattern consists of three components:

1. **Cue:** Anything that triggers a behavior. It's the thing that tells your brain to cruise on autopilot.
2. **Routine:** The behavior that you want to change or reinforce. It's the habit itself.
3. **Reward:** The positive reinforcement you get from engaging in the routine—generally something that satisfies a craving. It's the reason the behavior has become a habit.

The habit loop is at the core of every habitual behavior. The reason it's so hard to break a habit is because every time a specific cue precedes a specific routine, which is then rewarded, the connection between them is strengthened in the brain. Every time that specific loop plays out, the habit becomes more ingrained in the brain. This is why you'll sometimes hear habits referred to as "sticky." The longer you allow a bad habit to exist, the stickier it becomes! To transform your habits, you have to break the habit loop.

THE DIFFERENT CUES OF THE HABIT LOOP

Generally speaking, there are five types of cues that trigger you to initiate a habitual behavior: time, location/environment, preceding event, emotional state, and other people. The following are examples of habit loops and the type of cue that triggers them:

CUE	ROUTINE	REWARD
Getting home from work (time)	Go to the gym	Healthier body
Walking into the living room (location)	Watch TV	Relaxation
Finishing your morning coffee (preceding event)	Meditate for twenty minutes	Feel calm and centered
Feeling upset (emotional state)	Eat a tub of ice cream	Release of feel-good dopamine
Seeing your coworker go outside for a cigarette (other people)	Smoke a cigarette	Nicotine buzz

Knowing your cues is essential to breaking bad habits, and choosing cues that suit your lifestyle is part of forming new, good habits.

UNDERSTANDING YOUR HABITS

So what are *your* habits? More importantly, how are they affecting your current level of mental toughness? Ask yourself: How do you habitually respond to stress? Or things that are out of your control? How do you habitually talk to yourself? How do you habitually react to failure? Do your existing habits make you resilient and confident, or do they reinforce negative beliefs that only hinder your progress? Are they leading you down the path of success, or are they doing more harm than good?

Changing your habits to promote greater mental toughness will start with an awareness of your own habit loops and a solid understanding of your cues and rewards. Throughout this book there will be plenty of opportunities to identify, explore, and address your habits—both the good and the bad.

FORMING NEW HABITS

Using the concept of a habit loop and your understanding of your own current habits, you can begin to create habits that nurture greater mental toughness. The following sections explore different methods for forming new habits.

START WITH AN EXISTING HABIT

The best proven method for developing a new habit is to piggyback onto an existing one (essentially, using a current habit as a new cue). There are so many things that you routinely do every day without much thought at all...routine morning actions like getting out of bed, brushing your teeth, taking a shower, eating breakfast, walking to work, or any-time-of-day activities such as turning on and off the lights, going to the bathroom, entering or leaving a room or building, or getting into bed. The list is endless! Choose any of these actions and make it your cue. Then, determine what new habit you want to create and decide whether you'll perform this habit (routine) directly before, during, or after the cue.

Consistency and repetition are key to habit formation, so set yourself up for success by ensuring you will be able to practice frequently. Also consider using reminders like your phone alarm or calendar.

START WITH MICRO HABITS

Changing your ingrained habits can certainly feel challenging. Many people make the mistake of starting off too ambitious, leading to a greater chance of failure and likelihood that they'll eventually give up. But even the smallest, most seemingly insignificant habits can be very sticky. Remember this when you're trying to change any routine behavior, and don't be so hard on yourself! Instead, work with the science of habits, not against it. Research says that the key to making big behavioral changes is to start incredibly small—with micro habits.

A micro habit is a small component of a larger habit—so small that the action should require minimal effort or motivation to complete, and should take no more than a couple of minutes to carry out. The idea is that you practice a micro habit every single day, so that over time, it will slowly build on top of itself. Each baby step will move you that much closer to your larger goal.

For example, if you want to form the habit of doing one hundred sit-ups every day, start with one sit-up every day. Or let's say you have a goal of reading ten books this year. If you're not already in the habit of reading every day, start incorporating that into your routine. Instead of setting out to read one chapter each day, maybe start with one page and slowly add more pages over time. Eventually, you may find yourself reading twenty, thirty, or even more books each year!

FOCUS ON BUILDING ONE HABIT AT A TIME

Have you ever tried to do a bunch of things at once and got so overwhelmed that you either gave up or somehow got through it, but with less-than-stellar results? The saying "one thing at a time" might have helped you on that occasion, and it will also help while you're trying to build your mental muscles.

Forming new habits is hard work. Focusing on one habit at a time will reduce the chance of getting overwhelmed and increase the likelihood of getting really good at that one thing. Patience is indeed a virtue here, because it will take persistence and dedication to stay with it once the initial drive has worn off and you feel tempted to switch gears and try something else. Flex that patience muscle by keeping your efforts focused on one habit until you see improvements. Then you can start the process over again with a new habit.

BREAKING BAD HABITS

Breaking bad habits can feel a bit trickier than forming new ones. After all, every habit you have right now serves some sort of purpose. Each is fulfilling a need or providing you with a benefit, even if it's bad for you in other ways. Often bad habits are a way for you to deal with stress, boredom, or some deeper issue. Biting your nails, overeating, smoking, watching too much TV—all of these bad habits can fulfill your need to curb stress or boredom or distract from emotional turmoil. As such, they can be harder to eliminate.

Instead of struggling to cut a habit from your life, aim to replace that negative routine with a more positive one that provides the same (or similar) benefit. The routine is the only part of the habit loop you need to change! Use the same cue but substitute a different routine to achieve the reward.

First, you'll need to identify the cue and reward for the habit you're trying to change. It's especially important to fully understand your cue, because your habit is constantly being reinforced by it. Understanding why you need that reward in the first place is equally important, though sometimes it can be a deeper issue that may not be so obvious.

HOW SETTING GOALS LEADS TO SUCCESS

So you want to be tougher mentally—that's great! Some might call that a goal, while others would say it's lacking a few of the key characteristics of a goal. For now, let's call that your ambition (which is more like the desire to reach a goal). Unfortunately, it's not enough to just declare your desire and hope it happens. You have to have a strategy for achieving it…and then you've got to do the work.

And that's where goals come in. Goals are specific, actionable outcomes you desire for your future. They can pertain to any and all areas of your life, such as career, finances, family, health, personal growth, and more. The ability to formulate goals goes hand in hand with success. Goals act as a blueprint that helps you design your future. They allow you to translate your abstract dreams into something tangible. Without them, you lack focus, direction, and discipline…and, more than likely, motivation. By carefully considering precisely what you want to achieve, and strategically planning how you will make it happen, you're much more likely to succeed.

HOW TO SET AND ACHIEVE GOALS

One of the most common questions people have about goal setting is "Where do I start?" If you're in this boat, not to worry! The following steps for goal setting will take most (if not all) of the guesswork out of it.

1. **Develop a clear idea of what you want to accomplish.** Do some research if you have to. Determine what habits or behavior changes might be necessary to achieve this goal, and ensure that it aligns with your personal values.
2. **Use the S.M.A.R.T. method.** Increase your chances of goal attainment with the S.M.A.R.T. format detailed later in this chapter.
3. **Write it down.** Having your goal in writing will bring it to life. It also helps to hold you accountable to that goal. Be sure to frame your goal statement positively as opposed to negatively; for example, "I will _____" instead of "I will not _____."
4. **Break it down.** Make a list of every specific thing you need to do in order to achieve your goal.
5. **Create a plan and timeline for completing these smaller tasks.** Assess what tasks need to be done first and prioritize them. Stick to one task at a time versus trying to take on a number of tasks at once.
6. **Re-evaluate your goal on a regular basis.** Ask yourself if you're on track; if not, determine how you can change course.

Not only is greater mental toughness a goal in itself; part of being mentally tough means setting and sticking to goals that will bring you closer to your happiest, most successful future. Use the tips and insights found here (and throughout this chapter) to help you create and achieve goals—both within your larger, long-term goal of leveling up and for everything you desire in life.

S.M.A.R.T. GOALS

You can't research goal setting without coming across the S.M.A.R.T. technique—an acronym that stands for Specific, Measurable, Attainable, Relevant, and Time-Bound. This ingenious framework for setting goals has been the standard for many successful people. It turns vague goals into something more tangible. Check out the following details for what makes a goal S.M.A.R.T.:

1. **Specific:** Your goal should be specific enough that you'll understand the steps necessary to achieve it. Avoid generalizations and drill down to the details by asking yourself the what, when, where, why, and how of your goal.
2. **Measurable:** Determine the objective criteria you will use to keep track of your progress. What evidence will prove that you're making progress toward your goal?
3. **Attainable:** Is your goal realistic? Make sure you can reasonably accomplish your goal within a certain time frame.
4. **Relevant:** Your goal should be meaningful—aligned with your core values and what you most want to achieve in life. If you want something badly enough, nothing will stand in your way.

5. **Time-Bound:** Your goal should have a definitive end date, helping to motivate you and create a clear timeline for your action plan. Having a deadline will promote a practical and healthy sense of urgency to propel you forward.

Here is an example of a goal that is vague, lacking clarity and direction: "I want to be in a leadership role." Here's how to make it a S.M.A.R.T. goal: "I will land a management position in the marketing department of a reputable company within three months."

Here is the S.M.A.R.T. proof:

1. **Specific:** The goal of becoming a marketing manager at a reputable company is well defined.
2. **Measurable:** Progress can be measured by number of applications, interviews, and job offers.
3. **Attainable:** Assuming the person setting the goal is well qualified for the position and has a great résumé, this goal is realistic.
4. **Relevant:** The goal aligns with values of growth and development.
5. **Time-Bound:** A deadline of three months has been set.

Use the S.MA.R.T. method when creating all of your individual goals—from the goals that are aimed at building more mental toughness to goals for achieving anything you want in life.

WHAT NEXT?

You've discovered the characteristics of the mentally tough person, learned more about the benefits of leveling up your own inner strength, and explored how creating good habits, breaking bad habits, and setting goals will help you get there. It's time to start working those mental muscles! Almost. Before jumping into the exercises that follow, there are a few more things you'll want to keep in mind, as well as some helpful tools to have on hand in order to optimize your results.

First, if you haven't already completed an assessment of your current level of mental toughness, do so now. You will use this assessment as you work through the exercises, gauging what you may need to work on most. Also, recognize your own personal limitations, especially as they pertain to the few physical exercises in the book. If something doesn't feel accessible to you, skip it! The mental discomfort that may be required for personal growth is not the same as physical pain. Know your limits. They will not impact your ability to level up.

USING EXERCISES TO SET GOALS FOR HABIT CHANGE

Previously in this chapter, you learned a lot about habits and goals; now it's time to apply that knowledge. Through the exercises that follow, you will build your mental muscles by changing your habits and setting goals that are motivating and hold you accountable to the changes you wish to make.

If you are unsure which mental habits are holding you back, start with the exercise "Identify Your Worst Habits" in Chapter 9.

Once you've uncovered the unhelpful habits you want to eliminate, you can begin reflecting on what good habits you may want to replace them with. And if you already have some healthy habits in mind that you'd like to adopt, check out the "Aim for Incremental Change" exercise in Chapter 2 for a step-by-step guide to making micro habits work for you.

Truthfully, any exercise in this book can act as inspiration for changing or creating habits. Let's say that you're afraid of rejection, so you have a habit of not taking chances. When you complete the "Get Rejected" exercise in Chapter 10, you may realize how valuable it would be to make it a habit to put yourself out there in small ways. Or maybe you're struggling to keep your temper in check and you want to change that. The strategies outlined in the "Change Your Perspective" and "Try the Five-Second Rule" exercises in Chapter 5 can help you develop the habit of stopping to think before you act. You can use the information about goal setting in this chapter (and Chapter 2) to develop S.M.A.R.T. goals pertaining to these or any other habits you decide to adopt or change.

WHAT YOU'LL NEED

A willing attitude, an open mind, and a deep desire to improve are all important for making the most of the exercises in this book. You will also need:

- A dedicated notebook/journal and writing implement
- A calendar or scheduler

These additional tools will allow you to complete exercises, track your progress, reflect as you go, note any ideas or realizations you may have, and keep working those mental muscles regularly.

TIPS FOR LEVELING UP

As you work through these next chapters, keep the following tips in mind. They will help you make continual progress and bust through any obstacles to reach the next level of mental toughness:

- Make time and space in your life to complete these exercises.
- Be fully present and mindful as you do the work.
- Approach the exercises with a beginner's mind: Drop any expectations and preconceived ideas, and instead, approach them with an open mind and fresh eyes—just like a beginner.
- Complete the exercises in the order that feels right for you—from beginning to end, or by focusing on a chapter(s) or specific exercises that most resonate with your needs and current situation.
- Read through an entire exercise and all its steps before getting started.
- Amend an exercise where you see fit: These are suggestions, not the be-all, end-all of success.
- Try not to overwhelm yourself by taking on too many exercises at once. There will be some that you complete right on the spot and others that require your efforts over the course of a day, week, or even longer.

Above all, remember that a commitment to the process is the most fundamental component of leveling up. You don't become mentally tough overnight. The suggestions that follow are meant to be practiced. You're not going to complete one exercise in this book and become the toughest person you know. To personify inner strength takes patience and mistakes. After all, there's no better way to learn than through failure. Keep returning to the exercises that are the hardest for you until you've truly conquered them.

CHAPTER 2

EXERCISES TO SET GOALS AND BOOST MOTIVATION

Goals and motivation go hand in hand. If your goals aren't motivating you, it doesn't matter how much time you spend on your strategy—you're likely to lose momentum. How does this fit in with building mental toughness? The overarching goal in completing these activities is to level up! And you can achieve that by strengthening the different components of mental toughness. Setting goals and staying motivated are the roots of cultivating emotional resilience, building grit, maintaining patience and self-control, increasing optimism, confronting stress, forging self-confidence, improving self-awareness, embracing failure, and honing attentional focus. Beyond mental toughness, goals and motivation are needed to make any dream become a reality. Even desires as small as staying hydrated or keeping up with dirty dishes require setting an actionable goal and staying motivated.

This chapter offers simple but effective methods for using goals to increase mental toughness and get essential tasks done. You'll learn the importance of structure and routine, and how breaking down your goals into smaller, more digestible tasks can keep the momentum and motivation high. You will also celebrate these small milestones along the way so you're more likely to stick to your goals and achieve the success you're after.

Personal values help you clarify your life's purpose. They're not something to achieve; rather, they act as an internal compass and influence your choices. Values are simply the intangible aspects of life that are most meaningful to you.

You can think of goals as stepping-stones that move you toward your values. While goals may change, values are more consistent. Aligning your goals and values means that you're picking goals according to your internal compass. And you'll be more likely to stick with and achieve your objectives when they're aligned with your values. It's no coincidence that mentally tough people are so persistent and passionate—they choose goals that fuel their purpose! When the going gets tough, their values become their directives. They're motivated to make sacrifices because it will bring them closer to the person they want to be.

TAKE IT TO THE NEXT LEVEL

First, use the "Know Your Values" exercise in Chapter 9 to determine what your core values are. Write these down in your notebook. Then determine a few smaller/short-term goals and one or two bigger/long-term goals that are fueled by each value (try to stick to one value at a time so that your attention doesn't get fragmented). These can be goals you've had for a while or goals that are just coming to life right now!

Here are examples:

Value: Freedom
Short-Term Goal: *To land my first freelance writing gig*
Long-Term Goal: *To become a full-time freelance writer*

Value: Family
Short-Term Goal: *To contact my parents once a week*
Long-Term Goal: *To build stronger relationships with my family*

Commit these value-based goals to memory—or even better, write them out and keep them somewhere you can see them—and start making choices that align with them!

EXERCISE 2: CREATE A VISION BOARD

All successful companies have a clear vision of what they most hope to achieve—a larger purpose that provides direction and inspires and motivates their workforce. Without this foundational piece, they might get stuck. Wasted resources, low morale, and unclear objectives could result. The same is true for your life! How can you achieve your biggest dreams when you're not clear on what they are? Just like a company's vision, this larger picture for your life can bring clarity and help guide you to make the best choices that are aligned with your highest self. Having a vision will not only breathe life into your goals; it will also make it that much easier to get back up after a disappointment or setback.

If you don't have a life vision, it's time to get clear on it. Through thought-provoking questions, you'll discover what you're striving for in your life. A visual depiction of this future will help you keep it in mind.

TAKE IT TO THE NEXT LEVEL

For this exercise, you can either create a traditional vision board using photos, pamphlets, magazines, and a cork or poster board, or create a digital vision board online or through a phone app. Whichever way you decide to do it, this project can be a fun and creative source of motivation and goal setting!

The first step is to get clear on your vision: Focus on the big picture. Think of the long-term, significant goals that resonate with your values and get you energized and excited. What does your ideal life look like? For inspiration, answer these questions in your notebook:

- What matters to you in life?
- What are your hopes and dreams?
- What are you passionate about?
- What are the greatest things you wish to accomplish?
- What do you want to contribute to the world?
- What would bring more happiness into your life?
- What does your dream career look like?
- What skills do you want to learn?
- What kind of people do you want to be surrounded by?
- What kind of relationships do you want to have?
- Where do you see yourself in ten, twenty, thirty, and even forty years?
- How do you want people to remember you?

Next, look for visuals that represent your goals for the future and place them on your board. For the traditional version, you'll need scissors and adhesive to attach the images to your board. Online and app versions will have plenty of visuals to choose from. Include any positive affirmations that will help you reach your goals (see the "Use Positive Affirmations" exercise in Chapter 6). Simplicity goes a long way here—you don't want to overcrowd your board and lose focus of the big picture. To get the full benefit from your board, put it somewhere you can always see it, or purposely take a look at it often.

EXERCISE 3: BEAT PROCRASTINATION IN FIVE MINUTES

What's the difference between someone who's mentally tough and someone who isn't? For one thing, mentally tough people don't sit around and wait for inspiration or the perfect circumstances to get stuff done. They use proven strategies and habits to boost their motivation and achieve their goals.

Generally, motivation comes from a sense that you'll gain something in the end, whether it be intrinsic satisfaction or an external reward. Since you know it's going to take a long time to accomplish that big goal of yours, your brain might resist initiating action toward it and instead procrastinate with more immediately satisfying activities. It gets even worse, because the more you feed the procrastination monster, the more anxious you feel about putting off the work. The more anxious you feel about it, the stronger the urge to avoid it.

When you're procrastinating any goal, you have to make it easy to get started. The best way to do this is to relieve some of the pressure. Instead of thinking that you'll only feel a sense of satisfaction once your goal is completed, decide that it will be a great accomplishment just to start it. Once you finally begin, you'll feel good about yourself and you might even have some fun with the task.

TAKE IT TO THE NEXT LEVEL

Follow these steps to beat procrastination in five minutes:

1. Pick a substantial goal that you're having trouble initiating because it feels overwhelming. It may be that you have to reorganize your entire office or go through all your clothes and donate what you don't need anymore.
2. Set a timer for five minutes to work on that goal. It can be planning or physically taking action—absolutely anything that will contribute to your end goal.
3. You've accomplished your goal of getting started! Pat yourself on the back or give yourself a reward—whatever works for you.

You may notice that when the timer goes off, it feels easy to keep going and you don't want to stop. You've already done the hardest part, and you may be feeling some momentum from your progress. If this happens, then keep going! Use this exercise as often as you need, whenever you're having difficulty getting started with a goal.

EXERCISE 4:
DESIGN YOUR ENVIRONMENT

Your surroundings help shape your behavior in a big way. Mentally tough people know that in order to maximize their chances of success in anything, they need to operate in an environment that is conducive to achieving results. This is especially important at the beginning, when you're trying to form a new habit for success such as eating healthier or working out every day.

Are you set up to succeed—to stay in it for the long haul (whatever your "it" may be)? Whatever it is that you're striving toward, find the path of least resistance. Tweaks to your environment can make it easier to get started when you're lacking motivation, and they help you get things done with consistency.

TAKE IT TO THE NEXT LEVEL

In your notebook, create a chart like the following one, identifying any habits that you're trying to develop or goals you are trying to achieve. Is your current environment supporting or hindering your success? Consider what might be negatively influencing you in your physical space and come up with some creative tweaks. Make it incredibly easy for yourself to make decisions that are aligned with your goals on a regular basis.

DESIRED HABIT OR GOAL	ENVIRONMENT TWEAK
Stop binge-eating junk food	Remove all junk food from the house
Practice guitar regularly	Keep guitar visible in a prominent spot in the living room
Control portion sizes	Use smaller plates
Go for a jog every morning	Place running shoes and gym clothes next to the bed before going to sleep

Get to work on these changes and keep mental (or written) notes of any improvements due to these tweaks!

EXERCISE 5: AIM FOR INCREMENTAL CHANGE

Sometimes "go big or go home" just doesn't apply. It's great to dream big, but in order to achieve those dreams, you have to start small. Whether the desire is for self-improvement or some external objective, mentally tough individuals understand that incremental, persistent changes over long periods of time are the key to achieving lofty goals.

Say, for example, you want to become an author. If you've never written anything substantial before, sitting down and saying, "Okay, I need to write a novel now," would be an effective way to squash that dream. When you look at a project as one enormous undertaking, it can be overwhelming and create a lot of mental resistance. If you want to become an author, you have to start with the daily habit of writing something much shorter. Writing just one sentence a day and gradually increasing this by increments could be the road to your success in one year, five years, or ten years.

TAKE IT TO THE NEXT LEVEL

Decide on a big goal that is currently overwhelming you. Then:

1. Determine an incredibly simple action you can perform every day to aid in reaching this goal. It should be so small that you almost think it's not worth doing (e.g., writing one sentence).

2. To encourage consistency, piggyback this new action onto a task that you already perform every day without thinking (e.g., writing one sentence while drinking your morning coffee).

3. Track your progress using a simple "yes/no" list. In your notebook or calendar, enter a yes for each day that you completed the desired action and a no for each day that you didn't.

4. After a couple of weeks of consistent yeses, increase the action by a small increment (e.g., writing three sentences while drinking your morning coffee).

5. Continue this process of making small, incremental adjustments until you're satisfied that the habit will get you to your results.

By doing this exercise gradually, the habit will become part of your muscle memory.

EXERCISE 6: BUNDLE YOUR TEMPTATIONS

Tough people don't have superhuman levels of willpower. They sometimes struggle to stick to their goals too, but they use proven strategies to get their desired result. The tougher you are, the more intrinsically motivated you'll be. Meaning, you persevere because of forces inside of you—not because you're seeking external validation or rewards. While you're leveling up in all aspects of mental toughness, you're naturally developing your drive and sense of intrinsic motivation. But until you get to the place where you view overcoming a challenge or setback as the reward itself, you can use proven hacks to keep your momentum going!

One such trick is to use external rewards. The brain is wired to place more importance on present comfort than future success. This is why (for some people) it's much easier to eat a bag of chips while watching a favorite show than it is to go work out. It's not something to feel bad about; it's just another circumstance that gets between you and your goals. But what if you tried using this to your advantage? A technique known as Temptation Bundling (also Reward Substitution) has you tie two activities together— one that you *should* be doing, and one that you *enjoy* doing—to invoke the willpower to get your work done. Basically, you use something instantly gratifying to encourage you to do a task that's less gratifying now but will pay off in the future. It's effective because you don't have to wait for the reward: You get it while you work!

Here are a few examples:

- Indulge in some funny *YouTube* videos (reward) while folding the laundry (task)
- Get a pedicure (reward) while catching up on work emails (task)
- Eat your favorite snack (reward) while scheduling social media posts (task)
- Listen to a podcast (reward) while tearing down drywall (task)
- Have a coffee (reward) while tackling your writing assignment (task)

The key is not to allow yourself to access the reward unless you're working on the task. One does not happen without the other!

TAKE IT TO THE NEXT LEVEL

Use the following chart to fill in your own tasks and rewards. Once you're finished, determine which tasks and rewards can be bundled together. Test them out to see which work best when paired together, and then try to implement them in your everyday routine.

It can be very effective to use multiple bundles throughout the day, and even make a habit out of using this technique.

TASK	REWARD	BUNDLE	EFFECTIVE? Y/N

EXERCISE 7:
MAKE ACCOUNTABILITY YOUR FRIEND

Accountability is one of the strongest tools at your disposal when it comes to achieving your goals. Mentally tough individuals use accountability to their advantage, knowing that anyone who's ever succeeded in anything didn't do so alone. Wouldn't it be great if you could have an accountability coach without having to pay an arm and a leg? Well, you can!

TAKE IT TO THE NEXT LEVEL

Ask one friend, family member, or even coworker to help you stay motivated and on track. Let them in on a specific goal you're working toward, and set up some regular check-ins. You don't want to make this too difficult for your accountability buddy, so keep it simple. Decide on a time slot for your check-in and who will get in touch with whom. It can be a weekly phone call or a daily text, or perhaps both. To make this foolproof, make use of technology to set reminders. Keep the check-ins short and sweet. Let your buddy know where you're at with your goal and any difficulties or roadblocks you're experiencing.

Bonus tip: Offer to be an accountability buddy for them too! This two-way accountability can be extra motivating and effective.

EXERCISE 8: GET INTENTIONAL

Your intention is what feeds your motivation to see a goal through, so it should define your actions. Just as an interviewer would ask, "Why do you want this job?" (and that why is likely the main motivating factor for all the prep work that goes into an interview), ask yourself, "Why do I want to level up my mental toughness?"

Also consider where else you could use a strong, motivating *why*. Is there a lifestyle change you've been wanting to make but never actually got around to? Maybe you want to establish a morning routine like all those successful people you've been reading about. But they have their own reasons for waking up at five a.m. to run three miles. Simply picking the routine of someone successful and adopting it as your own with no compelling reason is not a good way to make it stick. If you want to revamp your morning routine so that you can feel more energized throughout the day, remind yourself of that reason every day, and allow it to drive your actions.

TAKE IT TO THE NEXT LEVEL
State your intention:

1. Think about why you want to level up your mental toughness. Your answer can be as simple or as detailed as you like, but make sure it's important to you.
2. Find a prominent space in this book to write down your answer. Whenever you're feeling low on motivation to do this work, turn to this page to remember your intention.

Where else would it benefit you to get clear on your intentions? Ask yourself the *why* questions and write the answers in your notebook so you can revisit them anytime your motivation wanes.

EXERCISE 9: CREATE A MORNING ROUTINE

The simplest way to stay motivated consistently is to eliminate the need for motivation! In other words, remove the hurdle of having to repeatedly summon the willpower to do something by making it a regular schedule or routine. A routine ensures your behavior is consistent and automatic and that you're never left wondering how or when you should get started. This efficiency frees up mental space to concentrate on more important things.

How many times have you heard about the routines of the world's most successful people? Most notably, the way they spend their mornings day in and day out seems to be of utmost importance. No matter what, they never compromise their routine. If you want to reap the full benefits of whatever routine you create for yourself, you've got to stick with it! Usually centered on productivity and health, a successful morning ritual lays the foundation for the rest of the day. Even more, it provides a sense of predictability and calm in a chaotic and unpredictable world. It's also the perfect opportunity to make sure you carve out time to pursue your passion every single day.

TAKE IT TO THE NEXT LEVEL

To develop a customized morning routine, first decide what it is you hope to accomplish. Is it important that you get a workout in or that you work on a personal creative project? Or do you want to use this time to organize your day? Determine the nonnegotiable(s) that you want to make time for every single day. For inspiration, here are some of the key elements of a successful morning routine:

1. It energizes you and wards off stress. Consider meditation, physical exercise, or positive affirmations.
2. It helps you gain clarity. Consider journaling, practicing gratitude, or setting intentions.
3. It helps you gain control over your day. Consider prioritizing your tasks, structuring your day, or planning your meals.
4. It allows you to carve out time for your passions/ personal projects. Consider reading, painting, playing an instrument—anything important to you that may easily get pushed aside as your day gets more hectic and demanding.
5. It helps you reach your goals. Consider working on your most important goal(s) for even just a few minutes.
6. It eliminates decision-making. Follow the same routine consistently at the same time every day.

The ritual of setting aside time for yourself every day will help you maintain the motivation to achieve more than you thought was possible.

EXERCISE 10: PRIORITIZE YOUR DAY

You've put so much thought into formulating your goals, deciding precisely what you aim to achieve. Now what? Now you have to strategically plan how you're going to tackle them. Structure and effective time management drive your objectives.

You know that one thing you've been meaning to do for a while now? Every day it seems to wiggle its way onto your to-do list but somehow never gets done. Why is that? Because you're not making it a priority! You have to plan your day in accordance with your top priorities—it's that simple. Start with your highest-value task, no matter how daunting or time-consuming it may be. Decide what that task is before the day starts.

TAKE IT TO THE NEXT LEVEL

For the next few days, try this method for prioritizing your daily tasks:

1. Before you do any work, review your current projects and get clear on what you need to accomplish.
2. List all the tasks you think you need to get done.
3. From that list, decide on your top three priorities for the day.
4. If there's anything on that list that is truly urgent and needs to get done right away, that's your first priority. Otherwise, ask yourself, "If I could only do one thing on this list today, what would it be?" Whatever that task is, that's your number one priority.

5. Repeat step 4 until you have prioritized your top three tasks of the day.

Now get to work on those three tasks, beginning with the most important. Only once you've accomplished your top three tasks can you start to tackle any of the other stuff from your main list.

EXERCISE 11: TRY THE 80/20 RULE

The 80/20 rule (also known as the Pareto Principle) states that 80 percent of your results (output) will come from just 20 percent of your actions (input). This principle was traditionally used as a business management tool to increase efficiency and effectiveness, but it's since been shown that this principle can apply to just about anything!

- 20 percent of criminals commit 80 percent of crimes
- The top 20 percent of earners pay 80 percent of income taxes
- 20 percent of patients account for 80 percent of healthcare spending

Don't get fixated on the numbers: It's certainly not always a 4:1 ratio, but this imbalance has been widely observed across many industries and circumstances.

When you take this rule and apply it to your own life, it becomes even more fascinating—and useful! You probably wear

20 percent of your clothes 80 percent of the time. And you spend 80 percent of your time with the same 20 percent of your friends and family. Twenty percent of your good habits are likely responsible for 80 percent of your rewards. Meanwhile, 20 percent of the tasks on your to-do list require 80 percent of your productivity.

TAKE IT TO THE NEXT LEVEL

Think about where this rule might apply in your life and write out a few of your personal 80/20s. What have you learned? What are the tasks that you need to focus on more in order to reach your goals? How can you optimize your energy for those tasks? Which are the tasks that are just busywork and proving little benefit? Find the 20 percent of your work that drives 80 percent of your results, and prioritize it!

EXERCISE 12:
SET GOALS FOR THIS WORKBOOK

Have you decided how you will make this workbook work best for you? Creating some of your own goals around how you're going to build mental toughness will help you level up, but it will also get you in the practice of setting and sticking to goals.

How you choose to use this book is up to you. Maybe you want to attempt one activity per day, or complete a chapter in one month. Make that aim a goal! Are there specific areas that you'd like to level up on? You can set a goal that has to do with building confidence, embracing failure, or practicing impulse control. And have you determined which of your least productive habits you want to kick? Establish a goal to ensure you're making incremental steps toward a behavior change.

TAKE IT TO THE NEXT LEVEL

Come up with a couple of goals pertaining to how you're going to use this workbook to level up. Don't forget to make them S.M.A.R.T.! You can come up with one or a few goals now, and maybe create a few more as you read through the book and discover other things you want to work on.

Here are a couple of examples:

1. I will complete three activities from Chapter 6 by October 1. This is S.M.A.R.T. because it is specific, you can measure success by the number of activities, it is realistic, it is relevant because you want to develop a more optimistic mindset, and it has a defined deadline.

2. I will prepare for my November 5 presentation by practicing visualization (using the "Visualize Success" exercise in Chapter 11) every day in the week leading up to the presentation. This is S.M.A.R.T. because it is specific, you can measure success by practicing seven times (one time every day of the week), it is realistic, it is relevant because you want to nail your presentation and be considered for a promotion, and the deadline is specific.

CHAPTER 3

EXERCISES TO CULTIVATE EMOTIONAL RESILIENCE

Emotional resilience is the ability to cope with life's adversities and bounce back after a difficult situation. It's an important element of mental toughness in which you understand and regulate your emotions, manage your thoughts, find meaning in unexpected challenges, and accept the things you cannot control. The more emotionally resilient you are, the more effectively you roll with the punches of daily life. The effects of resilience in one area of your life undoubtedly spill over into other areas as well. For example, becoming more resilient in the workplace also makes you more resilient in your personal relationships, and vice versa.

In the following exercises, you'll learn how to take back your emotional power and focus your energy on changing the things you do have control over, instead of dwelling on the things you don't. You'll define your emotions, explore what emotional responses are effective and what responses aren't, practice letting go of harmful thoughts and emotions, and cultivate a grateful attitude. As with every aspect of mental toughness, resilience can be learned and strengthened over time, so there's no excuse not to level up your emotional intelligence, tolerance for stress, and more. It's time to stop letting your emotions dictate your thoughts and behaviors.

EXERCISE 13:
BUILD YOUR EMOTIONAL VOCABULARY

Let's be honest: In order to have any control over something, you need to be aware of it. Understanding your emotions makes it much more likely that you'll be able to regulate them. Yet most people struggle to name the emotions they feel.

It's time to change that by giving your emotions distinct labels that help you define them. Labeling an emotion also allows you to create distance between yourself and the experience, giving you the opportunity to respond rather than react (an important attribute in mental toughness!) to what is happening. The words you choose to identify your emotional experiences can also impact the intensity of what you are feeling (providing relief) and help you recognize the source of your feelings. This leads to positive change!

TAKE IT TO THE NEXT LEVEL

Grab your notebook and set aside twenty minutes or so to complete the following steps:

1. Think about some of the experiences you've had during the past week. They don't have to be overly exciting encounters or negative or positive ones; just pick a few notable things that occurred. Perhaps you can look at an event that happened at work, a conversation you had with a friend, or a visit to a family member. Make a quick list of these experiences.

2. Go through each experience on your list and mindfully walk yourself through it. Write out in detail the emotions you felt during that experience. Where possible, try to come up with two or more words to describe how you were feeling at each point during the experience.

Following is a non-exhaustive vocabulary list of emotional terms to help you narrate your experience with greater emotional depth. Try using words that you don't normally use.

Curious	Exhausted	Melancholic
Agitated	Surprised	Nervous
Eager	Elated	Energetic
Apprehensive	Inspired	Content
Compassionate	Defiant	Adoring
Disapproving	Courageous	Distracted
Embarrassed	Disgusted	Outgoing
Relieved	Quarrelsome	Self-Assured
Sympathetic	Proud	Threatened
Uncomfortable	Trusting	Witty

3. Once you've completed these steps, take a moment to admire the breadth of emotions you've uncovered from this past week. Make note of any clarity you have gained about these experiences or through completing this exercise in general. Did you find it challenging to label all the emotions you felt this past week? Would it have been more difficult without the vocabulary list?

Feel free to practice this labeling whenever you can, whether in real time or in reflection. Remember that learning to label your emotions can help you become better at self-regulating, but as with all new skills, significant change requires practice and dedication.

EXERCISE 14: FILL YOUR CUP FIRST

Have you ever heard the saying "You can't pour from an empty cup"? It's a simple metaphor for making sure you take care of yourself. Your cup is empty when you're emotionally overloaded and drained by stress and other negative factors. But if you keep pouring—keep giving your time and energy to things and people—it will lead to complete burnout. Then you won't be able to help anyone, including yourself!

Your cup is full when your emotional, physical, mental, and social needs are met. You're well rested, nourished, energized, loved, connected, and productive. When you make yourself a priority, you're much more likely to have the emotional capacity to deal with whatever life throws at you.

TAKE IT TO THE NEXT LEVEL

It's time to refill your cup!

1. In your notebook or on a blank piece of paper, draw a cup. It can be a fancy Starbucks cup or the favorite mug in your kitchen cupboard. Make it big enough so you have room to "fill it up."
2. Inside the cup, write or draw things that fill your cup—that make you feel well. These can include reading a good book, hanging out with friends, getting enough sleep, doing something creative, and so much more.
3. Whenever you start to feel like you're running low on emotional energy, remember this image. You'll know what you need to do!

Cultivate the habit of checking how full your cup is and refilling it regularly.

EXERCISE 15:
STRENGTHEN YOUR SOCIAL SUPPORT

Your individual strengths are certainly crucial when it comes to having emotional resilience, but the role of social support is also huge.

To many, the word *tough* implies that you have to go it alone. The truth is, emotionally resilient people know how to reach out for help and proactively seek the support they need. They understand the critical role that supportive friends and family play in their overall well-being, especially during times of crisis. Social support can be any physical or emotional comfort, including help with finances or daily tasks, offering advice, or simply someone to listen or a shoulder to cry on.

TAKE IT TO THE NEXT LEVEL

This exercise will ensure you have the support you need when times get tough. If you can already name your social support network, fantastic! Continue to foster those relationships. Determine a few things you can do to strengthen your connection with each person.

If you're not sure who your support group is, bring to mind the people who care about you, think well of you, and want the best for you. Make a list of these people in your notebook. Remember that the quality of your support is much more important than the number of people you can write down. If you can come up with just two people, that's awesome! If you are still struggling to come up with a quality support network, you might want to begin fostering new relationships. Try volunteering in your community, finding clubs or groups that cater to a special interest, or going directly to a support group that suits your needs.

EXERCISE 16:
PRACTICE RADICAL ACCEPTANCE

Here's one thing that mentally tough people definitely don't do: Waste energy on things they can't control. Instead, they accept their reality and come to terms with things they can't change.

When you experience a negative event, the tendency might be to get upset and blame the situation on others, or to get caught up in regret and blame yourself. You might get stuck on the fact that this awful thing happened and wish you could go back in time and change it. Radical acceptance can help you release the energy spent on these uncomfortable thoughts and emotions, and make space for you to move forward.

TAKE IT TO THE NEXT LEVEL

Follow these steps to radical acceptance the next time you're struggling to accept a situation or if there's a situation from the past that's still haunting you.

1. **Ask, "What's the problem?"** Identify something that you're having a hard time accepting (past or present).
2. **Ask, "What caused it?"** Write down all the *facts* that led to the event. (Remember that facts are not the same as judgments! Try not to point to blame or make assumptions during this step.)
3. **Observe how you're feeling about the situation.** Since emotions physically manifest in the body, you may notice an increased heart rate, muscle tension, or sweaty palms. Or maybe you don't experience any physical sensations, but you feel sadness, shame, or anger. Be open to the full expression of whatever you're feeling. It may help to slow your breathing and sit in an open, accepting posture (shoulders back, heart toward the sky, arms open) during this step.

4. **Accept your feelings.** Whatever sensations arise in your body and whatever emotions come up, *accept* them. Let go of thoughts and feelings that fight the reality. Try repeating a few statements of acceptance, such as "It is what it is," "Everything is as it should be," or "I can't change what has already happened."

5. **Make a plan for moving forward.** Mentally tough people constantly adapt to change without panicking. When things don't go according to plan, they make a new plan! Think about how you can improve the situation and move forward. If the situation hasn't affected you in a significant way, you can stop at step 4.

Moving forward can seem scary, but the alternative to getting stuck in regret and resentment is ultimately much worse.

EXERCISE 17: TRY THE OPPOSITE ACTION

Intentionally creating conflict and allowing outbursts of anger or passive-aggressive behavior are examples of overreactions to a situation. While most people are guilty of at least one of these from time to time, regularly employing these responses can reflect poor emotion regulation.

Emotion regulation is the ability to enhance or reduce an emotion as needed—adjusting the intensity of it, when you have it, or how you react to it. It helps you control impulsive behaviors and act appropriately in different situations. Examples include redirecting your thoughts to reduce feelings of anger (downregulation) or looking for the good in a situation to increase feelings of happiness (upregulation). While both are important, knowing how to regulate your negative emotions in particular can be crucial in promoting resilience.

TAKE IT TO THE NEXT LEVEL

For each of the emotions listed in the following chart, write down the reaction that you would typically have, then determine if you think that behavior is effective in the long run. If your answer is no, describe what the opposite action would be. Feel free to list more than one behavior for different emotions or even to get more specific with them. The idea is not to invalidate the reality of what you're feeling, but to positively transform the way you react to what you're feeling.

In addition to arming you with positive options that will support your goals rather than hinder them, the aim here is to get you thinking about whether or not you need to work on your emotion regulation. You be the judge!

EMOTION	BEHAVIOR	EFFECTIVE IN THE LONG TERM?	IF NO: OPPOSITE ACTION
Sad	(e.g., withdraw from loved ones)	No	Reach out to loved ones
Anxious	(e.g., take a moment to breathe and collect myself)	Yes	N/A
Angry			
Scared			
Annoyed			
Lonely			
Guilty			
Ashamed			

EXERCISE 18: LEARN TO LET GO

Do you have a hard time letting go? When you hold on to resentment or something negative that happened to you, it keeps you stuck. The harder you attempt to cling to past experiences or ideas about how things should be, the harder it is to be fully present, where life is actually happening. You miss out on experiences and opportunities in the here and now—and the happiness and success they can bring—by dwelling on what has already happened.

Mentally tough people don't dwell on the past or stress about the future; they know how to live in the present moment. And if you want to be mentally tough yourself, you have to get unstuck!

Letting go is an active process. You will need to practice it regularly to build it into an automatic reaction. And meditation is a great place to start. Meditation teaches you to quiet your mental chatter—the space where your attachments to the past (and anxieties about the future) live. Through meditation you can begin releasing these attachments and accepting your reality as it is—regardless of how sad, angry, or hurt you might be from your past experiences. This emotional acceptance will enable you to adapt and get on with your life.

TAKE IT TO THE NEXT LEVEL

Identify one or more things that are no longer serving you and write them down using this format: "I am ready to let go of _____." Examples of things that may not be serving you include:

- Painful feelings
- The need to control things
- A past event
- A relationship
- A destructive habit or pattern

Once you have your list, prepare your body for meditation. Make sure you're comfortable, whether sitting or lying down, and allot yourself at least five minutes of quiet, uninterrupted time. Then:

1. Begin to focus on your breath—and nothing else. Thoughts will come and go; let them. Just try to focus on your breath and not the chatter.
2. Bring your attention to the first item on your list. Keep this item in your mind as you close your eyes and continue your focused breathing.
3. Exaggerate your exhales. Visualize yourself letting go of this thing that is no longer serving you—releasing it with your exhaled breath. Imagine yourself energetically expelling this resentment, pain, pattern, and so on from your body.
4. Breathe through your list. Repeat steps 3 and 4 for each item.
5. Say a final goodbye. Tear up the list into tiny pieces and say goodbye to it as you throw it in the garbage.

You can perform this exercise anytime you're feeling stuck on the past and you know you need to move on.

EXERCISE 19:
KNOW YOUR EMOTIONAL BLIND SPOTS

Similar to a physical blind spot while you're driving, an emotional blind spot is an obstructed view of an emotional area in your life—something you're unaware of or have chosen to ignore because you're afraid of where it may take you. And what you can't see can be hazardous. Generally, these blind spots involve emotions that are troubling or frightening, and that might challenge the way you see yourself and/or the world around you. Avoiding these feelings because of where they may take you is a form of denial, because whether you realize it or not, these feelings will dictate your thoughts and behaviors and drive your decisions. And oftentimes, this denial only compounds the uncomfortable emotions (e.g., feeling ashamed about your sadness).

Shutting people out, being unwilling to accept blame, avoiding conflict at all costs, or always needing to be in control are some examples of ways that people might avoid difficult or confusing emotions. In order to be resilient you need to acknowledge your true feelings and experience them fully. Only then can you truly let them go and move forward.

TAKE IT TO THE NEXT LEVEL

This exercise aims to identify and remove your emotional blind spots. Remember to be gentle with yourself while working through these steps. After all, everyone's got blind spots from time to time; you just need to adjust the mirror. Grab your pen and notebook and reflect on the following:

- Do you have repetitive experiences in your life that leave you asking, "Why does this always happen to me?" Identify areas of your life in which you find yourself asking that question.
- Do you avoid things that make you emotionally uncomfortable?
- What's the one thing you least want to accept?
- In what ways have others described you that you didn't quite agree with or couldn't make sense of?
- Are there any emotions from past or present experiences that you haven't felt completely?
- Are you consistently getting into the same type of unfulfilling relationships?
- What are you afraid to know?

Hopefully after pondering the previous questions, you'll be more aware of emotions you may be choosing to ignore in your life. Take a good look at these insights and think about how you might work through these uncomfortable emotions next time instead of blocking them out. It's not uncommon for more insight to come to you in the days and weeks following this exercise, so stay alert and be open to any breakthroughs.

EXERCISE 20:
MAKE GRATITUDE AN ATTITUDE

Mentally tough people consciously cultivate gratitude regularly, knowing that it will help cushion the fall when something undesirable happens. A grateful mindset enables you to keep your focus on the bigger picture and draw from all the resources and good things in your life. Instead of feeling overwhelmed or discouraged by a difficult situation, the bigger picture helps you feel confident that you have the tools and ability to not just weather the storm but thrive in it. Focusing on gratitude promotes openness, optimism, and creativity—all useful for navigating tough circumstances. And unlike events outside yourself, which often can't be controlled, an attitude of gratitude can be chosen, regardless of your circumstances.

TAKE IT TO THE NEXT LEVEL

Think back to a difficult time you went through. Who did you lean on for support? Make a list of those people who helped you get through this time. Then write a thank-you note to each of these people! They can be handwritten notes, emails, or even text messages—it doesn't matter. The notes can be as long or as short as you want, as long as you express your heartfelt gratitude.

By thinking back to these trying times and realizing that you got through them, you can choose to be grateful for what they taught you, grateful for whomever helped you through, and grateful that you came out the other side. By making this or any other type of gratitude practice a regular part of your life, you will begin to find gratitude more naturally in moments of great difficulty.

EXERCISE 21:
TRACK YOUR MOOD

Unlike emotions, which are a result of specific events or situations, moods are more like an overall state, often blossoming for no apparent reason. They influence the way you interpret and react to things in a big way, and can persist much longer than emotions. If you're someone who is generally positive and optimistic, your feedback loop would likely perpetuate your good mood; while someone who's in a low mood would be more inclined to interpret and react to a situation negatively, prolonging the experience of the negative mood.

When you're stuck in a negative feedback loop, it can feel like your emotions are controlling you, but there *is* something you can do about it! Instead of reflecting on your mood in hindsight, keep track of your emotions and mood patterns in the moments they occur to give you a more immediate understanding of where they're coming from.

Mood tracking can bring a welcome clarity to why your mood has changed so drastically or persisted for so long. It will help you discover the connections between your emotions, thoughts, and the situations you're in. Staying attuned in this way means you'll be able to recognize warning signs and the people or places that may be triggers. It can also be a very motivating experience when you realize that you can have an impact on your own mood.

TAKE IT TO THE NEXT LEVEL

When tracking your emotions, get as detailed as you like. Use your notebook or download one of the many apps that make it super easy to track your mood and activities on the go. If you're more of a visual person, you may prefer apps that use emojis and symbols instead of words. Find a method that works for you. The important thing is to keep track for at least a couple of weeks so that you have enough data to notice patterns or trends in your mood.

Throughout this exercise, record the following data in your notebook using a chart like the one that follows. Some of this information is best to record in the moment, while you may want to allow for the space of a few hours, or wait until the end of the day, to answer other questions.

After a few weeks, reflect on any patterns you may recognize. What may be triggering certain emotions? Is there something you can do to reduce or eliminate your exposure to these triggers?

DATE & TIME:	THE EMOTION WAS:	THE EMOTION WAS CAUSED BY:	BEHAVIORS/ ACTIONS THIS EMOTION LED TO:	WAS EMOTION APPROPRIATE TO THE SITUATION?	IS THE SITUATION OUT OF MY CONTROL, OR IS THERE SOMETHING I CAN DO?	OVERALL MOOD AT THE END OF THE DAY:

EXERCISE 22:
ADAPT TO CHANGE

It can be painful and difficult to accept a tragedy or unexpected loss. The tendency is to shut down in the face of this kind of change, but fighting against it is like trying to swim against a rip current. The best course of action is to ride the change like a wave: Try your best to adapt to the changing tides.

Fortunately, human beings are one of the most adaptable species on the planet! They can adjust to new conditions and cope with change—even capitalize on it. When unforeseen events completely alter their life plans, they adjust. There's no escaping the impact that change can bring into your life, but it's useful to be aware of how you generally adapt to big changes—what works well and what doesn't—so you can nurture those skills that help you bounce back emotionally from unexpected shifts, and re-evaluate the reactions that make resilience more difficult.

TAKE IT TO THE NEXT LEVEL

Grab your notebook and take some time to reflect on all the ways you were able to adapt in the face of a major loss or adversity. Specifically, how did you cope and roll with the punches? Did you have a support system? If so, was it beneficial? What was the hardest part of adapting? What did you learn or take away from the setback? What is/was life like afterward? How you adapted to this specific incident will inform your best practices for adapting to the next one. Never underestimate the power of self-reflection.

EXERCISE 23: TRY EXPRESSIVE WRITING

After suffering a traumatic or painful experience, people often block out those memories and negative emotions as a way of regulating their mood. But suppressing a painful experience causes more harm than good. Blocking out emotions puts stress on the mind and the body, encouraging symptoms such as anxiety, depression, headaches, autoimmune disorders, and more.

Expressive writing is one of the best ways to deal with overwhelming emotions, because translating an emotional experience into actual words makes the experience easier to grasp and can bring clarity to a situation. It's also been known to improve happiness and lead to positive behavioral changes. In the safety of your own private notebook, you can facilitate your own healing and build emotional resilience by expressing anything that's been too difficult to bear.

TAKE IT TO THE NEXT LEVEL

For this exercise, you'll use your notebook to write about a very difficult experience that you may not have fully processed or healed from. This can be the death of a loved one, serious illness, rejection, or failure—any negative event that you've struggled to move past.

1. Set aside twenty minutes to go somewhere quiet where you can be alone and write.
2. Recall the difficult experience and allow your thoughts and emotions to spill onto the paper. With no regard for

grammar, spelling, etc., explore your thoughts and emotions surrounding what happened and how it's affected your life.

3. Write continuously for twenty minutes. If you feel you've run out of things to say, you can recap what you've already written.

This exercise is purposely going to bring up a lot of emotions. Recognize that it's okay to feel sad or disheartened during and after writing, and that these feelings will fade as the day goes on.

EXERCISE 24:
PUT AN END TO EMOTIONAL EATING

Emotional resilience is a skill you have to continually cultivate. While some of the factors involved might be more obvious—like emotional intelligence and building a support system—others are often overlooked. For example, lifestyle choices that support your immune system are equally important for your mental health. Eating healthy, nutritious foods such as avocados, bananas, citrus, cruciferous vegetables, oily fish, and whole grains will help you build resilience so that you aren't as affected by stress.

Ironically, during difficult times it's common to crave the exact foods you should be staying away from. Emotional eating is when people turn to food to help them deal with stress or other unwanted feelings. It's a coping mechanism that might work in the short term, but exacerbates the issue long term. The usual "comfort foods" like sugary, fried, or processed refined foods actually weaken the body's ability to respond to stress!

While emotional eating can feel difficult to control, it is not impossible. It starts with awareness and facing emotions head-on.

TAKE IT TO THE NEXT LEVEL

If you suspect that you may struggle with emotional eating, use the following questions to guide your inquiry. In terms of your eating patterns when dealing with stress or other difficult emotions, consider these questions:

- Does your hunger come on quickly or gradually? (Emotional hunger tends to hit quickly.)
- Do you crave specific foods? (Emotional hunger is usually associated with cravings for specific, unhealthy foods.)
- Does the hunger come from your stomach or your head? (Emotional hunger starts with thoughts, not a rumbling stomach.)
- Do you have feelings of regret, shame, or guilt after eating? (Satisfying physical hunger is usually not associated with negative feelings; emotional eating is.)

The next time you start craving junk food and suspect it has more to do with your emotions than actual hunger, try the following:

1. Rate your physical hunger on a scale of one to ten, then rate your emotional hunger on a scale of one to ten. If your emotional hunger rating is higher than your physical

hunger, move to the next step. Otherwise, go ahead and grab yourself a snack!

2. Label your emotion in the moment. Are you lonely? Sad? Stressed? Angry? Overwhelmed?

3. Try to identify times when you've experienced this uncomfortable emotion before and what healthy coping strategies may have worked. If you're not sure, ask yourself, "What do I need right now?" You may want to complete the "Establish Healthy Coping Strategies" exercise in Chapter 7, and then return to this exercise.

4. Try one of these coping strategies instead of reaching for junk food: Take a bath, phone a friend, do some meditation or yoga—at the very least, get up and shake it out.

5. Begin the process of reframing what "comfort food" looks like. In times of stress, magnesium, vitamin B, and vitamin C are some of the first nutrients to get depleted. Natural, whole, unprocessed foods containing these nutrients are actually what your body needs—not junk!

CHAPTER 4

EXERCISES TO BUILD GRIT

Grit is made up of five characteristics: courage (to confront grief or uncertainty), conscientiousness (to work diligently and take obligations seriously), perseverance (persistence despite difficulties), mental resilience (the flexibility to adapt in a crisis), and passion (a strong desire to pursue long-term, meaningful goals). Together, these traits create an unyielding spirit essential to mental toughness. You might think of grit in terms of extreme situations, but you can actually build this inner strength through small wins every day. The gritty person understands that life is a marathon, not a sprint, and they approach each waking hour and aspect of their world ready to put in the effort it takes to succeed.

The exercises in this chapter will help you level up your grit—and therefore your mental toughness—by focusing on incremental improvements in each of grit's main characteristics: courage, conscientiousness, perseverance, resilience, and passion. You'll learn to embrace discomfort, complete unfinished projects, ditch perfection in favor of progress, commit yourself to long-term challenges, discover passions, and more. It's time to take the next step in building true inner strength.

EXERCISE 25:
FINISH WHAT YOU STARTED

Who isn't guilty of starting something they never finished? It's not always a bad thing. Some things don't quite pan out the way you thought they would, and after some assessment you decide not to continue. The problem arises when abandoning projects starts to become a disruptive pattern in your life. The instrument you bought and played for a week is now collecting dust. That website you started to create last year is sitting unfinished. The stack of books accumulates on your nightstand, each with just a few chapters read.

Not following through with these things may seem harmless, but a persistent habit of not completing things will quickly become your default. When it comes to achieving your biggest goals, it's likely that you'll face some sort of resistance or obstacle along the way, and if your habitual response is to give up, how are you going to accomplish what's most meaningful to you? Grittiness enables you to persevere despite difficulties or boredom! It is an essential element of success.

TAKE IT TO THE NEXT LEVEL

Recall a recent undertaking that you began with gusto but didn't complete, or a project that you neglected a while ago. Either way, you're going to assess the situation to determine where things went wrong and whether or not this is something that you actually want to finish.

Grab your notebook and begin to write about the experience using the following prompts:

- Was it something you felt passionate about?
- Were you intrinsically motivated to complete it? (It's easier to stick with things that are intrinsically rewarding.)
- Were your expectations for this project realistic?
- Were you aware of potential obstacles?
- Did you have a clear-cut plan for getting to the finish line?

After you've taken time to answer these questions, determine if the project is something you'd really like to finish. If it isn't, ask yourself why. Is it because you're lazy or lost interest, but the project would still be beneficial to your life? Or does it legitimately make sense to abandon it? If it is something you'd like to finish or feel that you should finish:

- Make a commitment to yourself that you will finish this time.
- Create a plan with actionable steps.
- Determine potential roadblocks you may encounter and decide how you will handle them.
- Get started and don't give up until you've completed your goal!

The next time you want to throw in the towel, take yourself through the previous steps and make sure you can justify it to yourself. By implementing this simple system and making a conscious decision to quit—as opposed to just walking away without any thought—you ensure that "giving up" is no longer a default behavior.

EXERCISE 26:
GET OUT OF YOUR COMFORT ZONE

People naturally tend to live within a comfort zone because leaving that zone increases anxiety, risk, and vulnerability. But did you know that discomfort is one of the biggest catalysts for growth? Think about it. If you're doing the same old thing, following the same routine, operating on autopilot—where is the opportunity for you to further develop yourself? Growth comes from the willingness to take chances and to feel awkward and uncomfortable when trying something new. The gritty person has the discipline to do what's uncomfortable when it's for the greater good of accomplishing their goals.

When you think of the word *uncomfortable*, what comes to mind? Is it public speaking? Telling someone a difficult truth? Or maybe it's the thought of getting back into the dating scene or trying something you've never done before. It's time to accept these feelings of discomfort and not let them control you! The more you practice, the easier it gets.

TAKE IT TO THE NEXT LEVEL
In this exercise you're going to choose something that makes you uncomfortable—either physically or emotionally—and you're going to go out and do it! Here are some ideas:

* Write with your opposite hand (whether for a journal entry or an entire day)
* Let yourself get hungry between meals
* Ask someone out on a date

- Take a freezing-cold shower
- Have a difficult conversation

Bonus points if you choose something that you know will be rewarding!

EXERCISE 27: TRY FOAM ROLLING

The grittiest people make a regular practice of getting comfortable with being uncomfortable. Why? Because sometimes the most uncomfortable situations can be the most rewarding—like having a difficult conversation with a friend that ultimately brings you closer together, or delaying gratification and waiting for something better.

Developing grit is all about this mindset of approaching discomfort with tolerance. If you train your mind to tolerate uncomfortable moments, you can call on that mental muscle when it counts—and be tougher for it. By fully immersing yourself in the act of foam rolling, for example, you can train your mind to not immediately stop when something feels unpleasant. What is foam rolling, you ask? It's a type of self-massage that alleviates tightness in the body. Benefits include increased mobility, blood flow, relaxation, and muscle recovery. Though it shouldn't be painful, some level of discomfort is to be expected.

TAKE IT TO THE NEXT LEVEL

For this exercise, you'll need access to a foam roller and the Internet. You can borrow a foam roller from a friend, try it out at a fitness center, or purchase one online. Alternatively, you can create your own by using a lacrosse or tennis ball.

Now, head to Healthline.com and enter "foam rolling" in the search bar—or if you're using a ball, search for "muscle release." Here you'll find the exact instructions for foam rolling, as well as the risks, benefits, and routines you can try. Much like everything in life, the general rule for foam rolling is that the places you feel the most discomfort (the "sticky" parts) are where you should focus your efforts.

After you've practiced this exercise for a while, consider how else you can commit to pushing your limits.

EXERCISE 28: UNCOVER DANGEROUS DISTRACTIONS

Stick-to-itiveness is the ability to stay with a project and see it through to completion. This type of dogged perseverance is one of the many impressive traits of a gritty person. But how do gritty people stay so dedicated to their work? By bringing focused attention to their chosen area of interest and avoiding distractions!

Distractions come in many forms. Some are obvious, like vibrating smartphones and social temptations, but others are not so obvious—they may not even seem like distractions at all. Tasks that are seemingly important have a way of keeping you busy, but busyness isn't always productive. Gritty people remain focused on the tasks that will get them closer to fulfillment and recognize that the busywork is just a distraction.

Thought leader James Clear said it best: "The most dangerous distractions are the ones you love, but that don't love you back." Do you know what your busywork is?

TAKE IT TO THE NEXT LEVEL

The following is an adaptation of Warren Buffett's strategy for maximizing focus and mastering priorities. Use your notebook to complete the following steps:

1. List your top twenty goals. This is purposely vague so that you can make the exercise your own. You can go big and list your top twenty life goals, or list the twenty things you most want to accomplish this month or even this week.

2. From that list, select your top three goals—the ones that are most important to you. Take your time with this step!

3. Now separate your top three goals from the other seventeen goals by making two lists. Both of these lists will be very useful, just for different reasons.

4. Label the list of your top three goals as such. Label the other list "Avoid at All Costs!" These are your most appealing (and dangerous) distractions that will keep you from accomplishing your important goals! Get familiar with this list and keep it readily available so you can remind yourself of it regularly.

5. Work diligently to achieve your top three goals.

6. Once your three top goals are completed, repeat this process. You might assume that you should pick three items

from the remaining seventeen, but you'd be surprised how much your priorities and interests could change once you've accomplished your top three goals.

EXERCISE 29: COMMIT TO THE CHALLENGE

Why is it so hard to follow through on your bigger goals, even when they're meaningful to you? Because sticking with something that might not be very enjoyable or immediately gratifying doesn't come naturally to most people. Whichever way you slice it, the journey between point A and point B is work.

Gritty people do not shy away from work. They don't expect any achievement to be handed to them. Instead, they commit to the process and understand that consistent, persistent action is the only way to their goal. They commit to making mistakes, failing, and getting back up. In fact, they actually get excited by the prospect of a challenge. They see it as a tool for growth, which makes it easier to do the work.

TAKE IT TO THE NEXT LEVEL

For this exercise you're going to create a challenge for yourself that will require long-term commitment to the work.

Here are the guidelines:

* It's up to you to decide what constitutes "long term" for the purpose of this activity, but aim for at least thirty days
* There must be a definitive end date

- It should relate to something you're passionate about; something you're willing to "suffer" for
- Make it achievable, not impossible
- You must have some way of being accountable for completing the challenge
- There must be some sort of structure or routine to ensure you're making progress

The following are some examples of challenges, along with how you could hold yourself accountable (A) for completing them, and the basic structure (S) for how you'll make time for them.

Run a marathon
- A: Register for the marathon and tell friends and family you're going to run it
- S: Run for x minutes or x miles every day before work

Complete an online course
- A: Sign up and pay for the course
- S: Complete one lesson/element of the course every day

Complete a thirty-day meditation challenge
- A: Sign up online and enlist a friend to do the challenge with you
- S: Meditate every morning when you wake up and text your friend when you're finished

Reflect on the challenge once you've completed it. How do you feel about yourself? How has it impacted your life? Would you do another challenge like this?

EXERCISE 30:
GET PREPARED TO PERSEVERE

At some point while working toward something meaningful, you may lose your momentum and even get discouraged. It can feel difficult to stay devoted to the task when gratification (a.k.a. the end reward) is delayed, so you need to have a plan in place for when this happens. To persevere, you need a strategy! How will you approach this endeavor? Do you know where you're going to do the work? Do you suspect you'll need to put boundaries in place, such as saying no to spending time with friends and loved ones? Remember that losing momentum doesn't make you a failure—it makes you human.

TAKE IT TO THE NEXT LEVEL
Using either an existing long-term goal or a new one, you're going to plan for the long haul. The aim here is to devise a big picture plan with some structure, and to prepare yourself for the roadblocks that may lie ahead.

Use your notebook to reflect on the following:

- Are you ready to make this commitment?
- If the answer to the previous question is no, what will make you feel more ready?

- What is the deadline?
- What is your timeline for doing the work, and is it sustainable?
- What are the milestones (or short-term goals) that will keep you on track?
- What method will you use to track your progress?
- How much time will you dedicate to this goal each month (or week or day)?
- When and where will you do the work?
- What boundaries will you put in place?
- What will the work look like when you're starting out, and how will it evolve?
- What will you do when your motivation starts to wane?
- How will you hold yourself accountable?
- What are the potential barriers to success?
- What will you do if you hit each of these barriers?
- Who can you turn to for support?

Take your time with this exercise. You may want to take breaks between answering some of the questions and allow for more contemplation.

EXERCISE 31:
CHECK YOURSELF
BEFORE YOU WRECK YOURSELF

Working toward a long-term goal can take a toll if you're not careful. Sometimes these big ambitions come with a lot of expectations, both from yourself and from others. The result is burnout.

Burnout is the accumulation of unchecked stress over a prolonged period of time. Since you don't always notice the signs of burnout until it happens, the best way to prevent it is to understand the factors involved and take proactive steps. The characteristics of burnout include physical and mental exhaustion, irritability, loss of interest and motivation, disillusionment with other people, and feeling empty. "Overachievers" are at higher risk than most, but anytime you allow stress to build unchecked, you run the risk of burning out.

Not only can your productivity drop dramatically at this point, but the effects of burnout can also easily spill into all other areas of your life. It can kill your creativity; leave you feeling hopeless, cynical, and resentful; and lead to serious health problems. Gritty people maintain their discipline toward long-term goals by avoiding burning out at all costs!

TAKE IT TO THE NEXT LEVEL

If you suspect you might be reaching your breaking point, take the following steps before it's too late. The main thing is to avoid Band-Aid solutions and focus on strategies for lasting change.

1. Check in with your purpose. Finding the value in what you're doing can help you regain a sense of purpose and control.
2. Analyze your responsibilities. Are the demands being placed on you reasonable? Take an inventory to determine what's being expected of you and by whom. Let them know that your workload may be leading you to burnout, and see if there's anything you can delegate. Ask for help!
3. Find balance. If you have absolutely no time in your life for your family, social activities, or creative hobbies, there's something wrong. Check your priorities and learn to delegate responsibilities. The exercises "Establish Boundaries" and "Set Internal Boundaries" (both in Chapter 5) may be useful here.
4. Make time for self-care. Prioritizing your wellness during times of stress is a very important preventative measure. Are you getting enough sleep, physical exercise, and proper nutrition? Do you have a stress-management plan? See the exercises "Customize a Self-Care Routine" and "Establish Healthy Coping Strategies" in Chapter 7 for some ideas.

Even if this exercise doesn't seem applicable to you right now, read through it so you have an understanding of how to avoid burnout in future times of stress.

EXERCISE 32: KNOW WHEN TO CHANGE COURSE

Sometimes when you're passionate about something and you've put your blood, sweat, and tears into it, you can suffer from tunnel vision, making it hard to see the signs that you should switch to plan B—or at least pivot a little bit.

Grit does involve finishing a job despite the challenges, but there's a fine line between working hard to get something done and complete burnout. To practice mental toughness, you need to be able to objectively assess your options and make hard decisions.

Changing course when you know it's the right thing to do does not mean giving up on your goal. It means adjusting your goal. You know the ultimate destination. Just because you might take a different route doesn't mean you're not going to get there!

TAKE IT TO THE NEXT LEVEL

Whatever long-term goal you're currently pursuing, do a quick assessment. What are your personal boundaries? If there are any thresholds you're not willing to cross—maybe in terms of finances, time, or stress—make yourself a plan B in case these boundaries are violated. Know the warning signs for when you should change course, and stay true to those boundaries!

EXERCISE 33: CREATE A PERSONAL MISSION STATEMENT

If mission statements are so important to organizations and leadership, why don't you have one for yourself? For the "enterprise" that is you? A personal mission statement defines who you are as a person and what your purpose is. Whether relating to your career or life in general, a mission statement explains in a measurable way how you aim to pursue your purpose, and also why it's so important to you.

Creating your own mission statement encourages you to think deeply about your life and clarify what is truly meaningful to you. Having this clarity can do wonders for your motivation—especially when striving toward something in the distant future—and your willingness to sacrifice comforts in pursuit of your purpose. Grit can be built through harnessing the power of your mission to tackle your highest goals.

Here are a few examples of mission statements:

- "Seeking to put God's love into action, Habitat for Humanity brings people together to build homes, communities and hope." —Habitat for Humanity
- "To be a teacher. And to be known for inspiring my students to be more than they thought they could be." —Oprah Winfrey
- "To organize the world's information and make it universally accessible and useful." —Google

TAKE IT TO THE NEXT LEVEL

Create your own personal mission statement, using the following questions to guide you. Keep it short, take your time with it, and make changes to it as you grow and evolve.

- What and whom do you value?
- What does your "personal best" look like?
- How do you want people to describe you?
- What kind of legacy do you want to leave behind?

EXERCISE 34: STREAMLINE YOUR LIFE

Mentally tough people are known to be "essentialists." They have very selective criteria for what they'll take on because they value their time and refuse to waste energy on what isn't important. When you say no to the things that are not essential for your success, you're saying yes to the things that are. You build grit when you practice this sort of sacrifice—giving up things that may actually be enjoyable so that there's more room for the essential stuff.

One of the ways you can begin to work on essentialism is to streamline your life. You hear a lot about minimalism these days—from simplifying your closet using tips from Marie Kondo's *The Life-Changing Magic of Tidying Up* to downsizing and living in a tiny home. The same idea applies here: When you simplify and streamline, you free up space for the most important things.

The first rule of simplifying your life is to identify what's essential and meaningful—what you're really passionate about.

Get clear on the purpose of what you're trying to accomplish, and remove anything that gets in the way of making progress toward your meaningful work.

TAKE IT TO THE NEXT LEVEL

For this exercise you're going to do a little spring cleaning. But instead of organizing the hall closet, you're going to "clean up" your life. The aim here is to build your grit—your ability to follow through on your commitments and persevere toward long-term goals—through focusing on what matters and tossing out the rest.

Evaluate the areas of your life you might be able to streamline (if you can think of more, great!):

1. Priorities: What matters most? What do you truly want to say yes to? What can you delegate?
2. Decisions: Where can you automate?
3. Consumption: What information is essential? What social media platforms are essential?
4. Schedules: Where can you make space for the unexpected? What can you decline?
5. Possessions: What physical clutter can you get rid of?
6. Communication: What e-newsletters can you unsubscribe from? What emails can you archive or delete?
7. Money: Where can you stop spending unnecessarily?

Now, get to it!

EXERCISE 35:
CHOOSE PROGRESS OVER PERFECTION

The path to success may present many internal roadblocks, and perfectionism is one of them. This personality style is characterized by very critical self-evaluations and by unrelenting, unreasonable personal standards of flawlessness. Perfectionists judge their self-worth based on achieving their impossibly high standards.

Having high standards for your work often produces great results, but at what cost? This mindset can have a terrible impact on your confidence and lead to extreme levels of stress. In contrast, gritty people prioritize steady progress and momentum over perfection. While they may strive for excellence, they know that mistakes are an excellent opportunity to learn and move forward. They appreciate the process and utilize the satisfaction of small wins to keep themselves intrinsically motivated.

Perfectionists miss out on this important aspect because they're so focused on the end result. Ironically, their pursuit of perfection will often keep them from either starting a project or from finishing it. Their assumptions or rules for themselves are ultimately unhelpful—inaccurate or inflexible in some way.

Many people have at least one area of life where they exhibit perfectionist tendencies. Do you?

TAKE IT TO THE NEXT LEVEL

Determine an area of your life where you've placed impossibly high standards on yourself. It's not always a conscious decision to be a perfectionist, so you might have to really think about this one. Where do you overplan, procrastinate, fail to delegate, give up too soon, or tell yourself that failure is not an option? It may relate to your performance at work, school, or in sports. It might also emerge in your close relationships, physical appearance, or fitness goals.

Once you've determined your perfectionist tendencies, write up the rules and assumptions you've built around them. Now consider how you can reframe your idea of success in these scenarios. Can you find satisfaction and pride in the small wins along the journey? Can you lower your quality expectation from "perfect" to "good enough"?

EXERCISE 36:
DISCOVER YOUR PASSION
THROUGH PURPOSE

"I don't know what I want to do with my life. What is my purpose?" If you've ever asked this question, you're certainly not alone. It's one of the big questions of anyone's life, and for good reason. A sense of purpose can keep you going during difficult times and is almost a prerequisite for the pursuit of lifelong goals. The more meaningful the goal—the more it is tied to your purpose—the more likely you'll be able to persevere through those mundane or monotonous moments.

The impact of purpose and how it correlates to performance has been thoroughly studied and accepted as a major predictor of success. But what about passion? Talk to anyone who possesses grit and you will undoubtedly learn what they're passionate about.

Passion keeps you interested and fuels your tenacity to continue pushing until you've reached your goals.

To better distinguish between passion and purpose, you can think of purpose as other-oriented—contributing value and making a difference in the world. Passion, on the other hand, is self-oriented—doing what you enjoy and what brings you satisfaction. Together, they are an unstoppable force for achieving true fulfillment and happiness. Think about the standard entrepreneurial success story. Someone sees an opportunity to fulfill a need (create value) for an underserved market. That's purpose! Over the years, they begin to enjoy their work because they take great satisfaction in helping their customers. That's passion!

If you want to improve your grittiness, drive, and stamina, pursue goals that are tied to both your purpose and your passion.

TAKE IT TO THE NEXT LEVEL
Use the following steps to uncover your purpose and passion:

1. Put all other thoughts and desires aside, and think about how you can create or contribute value today. In every single encounter you have for the next twenty-four hours—be it with friends, family, coworkers, or even strangers—find a way to create value for them. Serve some sort of purpose.

2. As you contribute and create value for others, start to cultivate awareness around when you specifically feel happy. What activities do you truly enjoy? What aspects of this service bring you the greatest sense of satisfaction?

3. Bring it all together. What did you learn about creating value for others? How did it make you feel? What did

you realize you're passionate about that you might not have realized before? Are these findings in line with the goals you've set for yourself? Where can you apply this information and optimize both purpose and passion in your life?

It's difficult to provide a timeline for this exercise, since discovering your purpose and passion is an ongoing process. Think of it as long-term, exploratory work.

CHAPTER 5

EXERCISES TO MAINTAIN PATIENCE AND SELF-CONTROL

A major part of success in any endeavor is merely the ability to stay the course. The unwavering pursuit of a significant goal involves two critical success factors: patience and self-control. Patience is the ability to wait for something that's beyond your control. Self-control is the ability to refrain from opting for sloppier quick fixes over lasting long-term solutions and to stick to the boundaries you've set for yourself. If you want to build a retirement fund, that means exercising patience while you watch your investments grow and control over impulse spending. If you want to lose ten pounds, you have to be patient with the process and have control over your eating habits. Someone who is mentally tough is disciplined. They know what they want and, more importantly, they're willing to exercise restraint in order to get there. They are patient with themselves and their journey.

The exercises in this chapter will get you to slow down and practice patience—mentally and physically. You'll learn how mindfulness facilitates more intentional behavior and discover what's really going on behind your own impatience. You'll draw from past experience to see that success doesn't happen overnight, and build self-control by implementing boundaries and strategies for delaying gratification.

EXERCISE 37:
PRACTICE BEING BORED

How often do you find yourself feeling bored? It's a generally unpleasant feeling characterized by a restless, unengaged mind. People often react to boredom by trying to immediately fill the gap with food, TV, alcohol, social media—anything to curb the unfulfilled desire for something satisfying.

But when you think about it, a certain kind of boredom is just impatience—anticipating what comes next, willing or even physically rushing it however you can. Mental toughness requires patience to wait for results and to endure monotonous work, practice, or training, day in and day out. After all, few things happen overnight! Progress toward any kind of success won't always be fun and exciting. Luckily you too can build the mental toughness to stick it out and conquer obstacles through the critical skill of embracing boredom.

TAKE IT TO THE NEXT LEVEL

The next time you're feeling bored, resist the urge to be stimulated and instead...just be. Don't whip out your phone or laptop, don't turn on the TV or check the fridge—don't even open a book. Sit with the boredom and feel it in your body. Notice what emotions emerge.

You can give yourself five minutes for this exercise at first and try increasing it each time you're bored until you are able to sit in boredom for extended periods.

EXERCISE 38:
TRY THE FIVE-SECOND RULE

How many times have you gotten yourself in trouble because you couldn't control an impulse? These unplanned, knee-jerk reactions have all sorts of consequences, whether it's taking unsafe risks on the road when the person in front of you is driving below the speed limit, coming home from the mall with things you don't have the budget for, or yelling at your child or partner for getting on your last nerve. When you're not in control of yourself, various areas of your life suffer.

If you struggle with impulses, you'll benefit from leveling up your mental muscles of patience and self-control. How do you train yourself to respond better in critical moments of temptation? Give yourself the opportunity to reflect before you act! This way, you'll be able to respond to the situation rather than react to it. The difference is that a reaction happens instantly and subconsciously (driven by biases and beliefs), whereas a response is more thoughtful and deliberate.

TAKE IT TO THE NEXT LEVEL

For one week, commit to using the five-second rule every time you're faced with an urge to react impulsively. Simply take five seconds to pause and consider your response to whatever the impulse is. Whether your trigger is an inconsiderate driver or a piece of cake in the refrigerator, pause for just five seconds and ask yourself, "Is this the choice I want to make right now?" A simple pause is often all you need to realize that your instinctual reaction is not in your best interest. Use your notebook to reflect on what you learned through this exercise.

EXERCISE 39:
ESTABLISH BOUNDARIES

In your relationships, what are the nonnegotiables (the limits you set with the people in your life to ensure that your needs are being met)? Boundaries make your expectations clear so that others know how you want to be treated. They make it easier to say no when you need to say no, and free you to say yes when you want to say yes! You are able to take personal responsibility for yourself and your priorities, supporting what you need.

Healthy, pre-established boundaries will help you maintain a level of control because they're rules you set for what can and cannot occur. Family members are often guilty of pushing boundaries, but others you're close to may step over the line as well. Here are some tell-tale signs that you need to set boundaries with someone:

- You feel taken advantage of
- You feel disrespected, insulted, or hurt
- You're being blamed for something you're not responsible for
- Your privacy is interrupted
- You feel that ideas, actions, or feelings are being pushed onto you
- You feel bullied, abused, or that someone is being too aggressive

You can't assume that people already know what you need. Instead, eliminate the guesswork by telling them what you need. And before you say yes to someone, make sure that it doesn't mean you're saying no to yourself!

TAKE IT TO THE NEXT LEVEL

Follow these steps for setting important boundaries with the people in your life:

1. Identify if there's anyone whom you might need to establish boundaries with. Use the previous list provided to help you. (If you can't think of anyone, that's great! At some point in your life, though, you may find this exercise to be useful.)
2. Identify what your boundaries are. It could pertain to an ongoing issue you have with this person or an isolated event. Examples include not communicating with someone if they are yelling and/or not allowing you to speak, and not answering client or coworker emails during weekends.
3. Communicate your boundaries clearly and calmly. Be direct; stick to the facts and avoid overexplaining or justifying yourself. If you'd like, you can emphasize that good boundaries strengthen relationships.
4. Expect that there may be some resistance and it might be uncomfortable. Don't let it discourage you. Avoid blaming or becoming defensive.
5. If your boundaries aren't respected, evaluate your options and decide your next course of action.

Recognize that this is an ongoing process and you may need to remind your loved one of your boundaries repeatedly. At first you might feel like you're being selfish or mean, but with time it will get easier. Your needs are valid, and you'll find that the more you respect yourself, the more others will respect you!

EXERCISE 40: DELAY GRATIFICATION

"But I want it now!" Sounds a bit like a toddler, doesn't it? Be honest, though: How many times have you been so impatient to satisfy an urge that you sounded like this? Whether or not you realize it at the time, you're choosing immediate gratification over a more desirable reward or outcome at a later time. Like making a big purchase that you can't afford and ending up with a massive credit card balance for months to come. Here, the more desirable outcome could be paying off your debt much sooner. Another example is hitting the snooze button a few times so you can stay in your warm cozy bed…at the expense of hitting the gym and eventually reaching your fitness desires.

The ability to control your behavior in the pursuit of long-term goals is one of the keys to mental toughness—and also one of the most valuable life skills. One of the simplest ways of exercising your self-control muscles is to practice mindfulness when faced with temptation. Get yourself out of "autopilot" behavior and into a place of self-awareness. However big or small the impulsive act, you're instinctually trying to satisfy a need. Identify the need, recognize your urges, and ask yourself if that need can be satisfied in a healthier way.

TAKE IT TO THE NEXT LEVEL

Determining what the underlying need is in the moment is a lot easier said than done. It's usually much easier to identify the need after the fact. So, for this exercise, you're going to work backward. The more aware you are of your automatic reactions to impulses in the past, the better prepared you'll be for them in the future.

1. Think long and hard about where you notice impulsive behavior in your life—behavior that makes you say, "I wish I had more self-control!"
2. Grab your notebook and write down situations in which you couldn't control your impulses and will likely struggle with them again.
3. For each of these situations, try to determine what the more favorable outcome would be if you were able to manage your impulse.
4. Now try to identify what the genuine need was in the moment that you gave in to the temptation.
5. Write down some other ways that you can satisfy that need in the future.

The next time you're faced with these impulses, practice mindfulness! As soon as you notice that urge coming up, slow down and assess what's going on. What is it that you really need in this moment? Return to this exercise and remind yourself how much better you'll feel about exercising alternative options.

EXERCISE 41: PRACTICE MINDFUL BEHAVIOR

Before you roll out of bed, do you find yourself instinctively checking your phone? When you're eating a meal, do you scarf down the food in an effort to get somewhere else faster, barely noticing the multitude of flavors and textures? This is mindless, habitual, "autopilot" behavior. In autopilot, you're less intentional about—and thus less in control of—your decisions.

The opposite of autopilot behavior is mindful, intentional behavior. Mindfulness means slowing down and focusing entirely on what you're doing, observing all the physical and emotional sensations you are experiencing in that moment. The practice trains the mind to become aware of and examine all emotions and impulses as they arise, teaches patience, and allows you the space to decide how you want to respond to the situation unfolding around you. It is a means of honing self-control that can be practiced every single second of every single day.

TAKE IT TO THE NEXT LEVEL

For twenty-four hours, practice mindfulness in all your typically habitual behaviors, including:

- Brushing your teeth
- Taking a shower
- Eating
- Walking

- Driving
- Cooking
- Working out

As you're performing each activity, devote all your attention and awareness to it. Engage all your senses! Try to notice everything you possibly can about the experience. For example, when preparing to brush your teeth, notice how the smooth toothpaste tube and the jagged cap feel in your hand. As you twist off the cap, do you hear anything? As you pick up the toothbrush, note the weight of it. Fully experience the act of squeezing the toothpaste out of the tube and onto the bristles. What do you smell? As the toothbrush enters your mouth, notice how it feels on your teeth, your gums, your tongue. Watch as the paste turns to bubbles. What can you hear? Experience the explosion of flavor. The simple act of brushing your teeth becomes a miraculous sensory experience if you just decide to pay attention!

At the end of the day, reflect on what you experienced. Do you see how mindfulness can teach you patience and stop unhelpful impulses in their tracks? Where else can you apply this practice in your life?

EXERCISE 42:
HAVE A REALISTIC TIMELINE

Cultivating greater mental toughness—and reaching any long-term goal—requires you to be in it for the long haul. This can present several challenges, one of which is the urge to do too much, too soon. At the beginning of your journey you'll probably have a lot of energy and motivation, which makes it tempting to attack the goal at full force. The problem with being overly ambitious at the outset is that you're likely to lose steam quickly.

This sort of impatience can sabotage your success. Instead, aim for consistent, incremental gains. It's great to be enthusiastic about your goals, but being realistic makes it much more likely that you'll achieve them. The other common pitfall when working toward a future target is the tendency to get bored and eventually give up—another reason why having realistic expectations about your progress is so important. As the old saying goes, "Success doesn't happen overnight." Work on shifting your mindset away from immediate gains, and appreciate the journey toward mental toughness.

TAKE IT TO THE NEXT LEVEL

This exercise will call on your past experience to show you just how crucial patience is for achieving long-term success. Grab your notebook and reflect on the following:

1. Consider your biggest accomplishment to date—for example, getting married, starting a family, receiving an award, starting a business, or landing your dream job.

2. Work backward to create a basic timeline of any big events or milestones you achieved along the way. Try to determine when you first set out to meet this goal.
3. Identify any losses, obstacles, or setbacks you experienced along the way.

Repeat steps 1 to 3 as many times as you like.

EXERCISE 43: CHANGE YOUR PERSPECTIVE

A lack of patience with another person is often caused by focusing too much on your own needs. There are two different scenarios where this commonly happens. The first is when you have an unconscious need that is manifesting as a different issue. Something else is bothering you, but you don't realize it, so you take out your frustration on someone else. For example: You're mad at your partner for leaving the dishes in the sink again instead of putting them in the dishwasher—or are you actually lashing out because you feel like they haven't been considering your needs or wants lately? You can think of this scenario as, "It's not you, it's me."

The second scenario is when you're so caught up in what you need that you fail to put yourself in the other person's shoes. For example: You're experiencing road rage because the driver in front of you doesn't know how to drive and it's going to make you late for dinner with friends. But what if the person in front of you has recently been in a car accident, so they're taking extra precautions to feel safer on the road? You can think of this scenario as, "It's not me, it's you."

Developing awareness of your impatience with others and considering a new perspective can help you let go of that frustration.

TAKE IT TO THE NEXT LEVEL

Look to your past to come up with a few examples of times when your impatience could've used a different perspective. Write out each example from your perspective, then consider the possible alternatives.

EXERCISE 44:
TAKE BACK CONTROL FROM YOUR SMARTPHONE

How reactive are you to your phone? A recent study sought to determine a link between impulse control and smartphone use. Not surprisingly, results showed that people with low self-control are more likely to check their phones as soon as they get a notification. Are you guilty of this?

Although compulsively checking your phone notifications may seem harmless, it's the pattern that becomes problematic. For one thing, it's a major drain on productivity. The context switching makes it difficult to get back into the zone of whatever you were originally focusing on. And being a prisoner to your notifications can make you look bad at work and in social situations, and even impact the quality of your relationships. In the worst-case scenario, giving in to your smartphone impulses can be deadly if you happen to be behind the wheel. A notification is your phone's way of letting you know that something new has happened so that you don't miss anything that might be worth your attention. But it's up to you to decide what's worth your attention at any given moment. It's time to take back control from your smartphone!

TAKE IT TO THE NEXT LEVEL

For this exercise you'll need your smartphone.

1. For three days, leave all your phone notifications on but do not open up your phone when you receive a notification! You must wait at least fifteen minutes before tending to it. (Use your best judgment to discern if something is truly necessary for work or other obligations, of course.)

2. After three days, assess how you feel about your smartphone use and if you want to do anything about it. How hard was it for you to delay the urge to check your notifications? Did it get any easier by the last day? What did this exercise teach you about impulse control?

3. If you dare, give your phone an overhaul and turn off any of the unnecessary notifications that are more of a distraction than anything else.

EXERCISE 45:
TEST YOUR OWN PATIENCE

If you're able to wait patiently for something, you have a healthful advantage over the average person. There are a plethora of triggers that may cause you to lose your composure throughout the day. For some, it might be an issue of patience with a particular person. Others have a low tolerance for delays and other daily hassles, such as waiting on hold for a customer service agent. The ability to wait calmly in the face of these hurdles is a learned skill in mental toughness that needs constant nurturing. Fortunately, you can use these moments of stress to develop more patience. Let go of what you can't control and accept that frustrations, setbacks, and wait lists are a part of life.

TAKE IT TO THE NEXT LEVEL

For this exercise you're going to pick a day to practice patience in every situation and with everyone you come in contact with. And it doesn't stop there: You're going to deliberately put yourself in situations where you'll be confronted with restlessness and frustration. It may help to plan out your day in advance.

As you go about your day, pay attention to what arises in you when your patience is tested—in your thoughts, your emotions, and your body. Following are some examples of ways you can practice patience, but you can get creative and customize your own list to suit your day environment.

- Drive in the slow lane or behind the slowest car
- Let people butt in line at the grocery store
- Take the longer route home from work
- Watch a movie that doesn't interest you

Before bed, use your notebook to reflect on the day and what insights you can take from this experience.

EXERCISE 46: CREATE AN IF/THEN PLAN

Impulsive behavior can be detrimental to your goals—and your path toward a tougher mind. Fortunately, you can avoid falling into this trap.

An if/then plan is a simple framework of alternative responses to certain impulses that challenge you. Also known as an implementation intention, if/then planning can help you prepare for situations that might derail you from reaching long-term goals (or forming new habits). It specifies when, where, and how you'll change your behavior in response to a common urge.

For example, if your desired outcome is to lose weight, it might look like this:

- If I want to binge-eat all the leftovers before bed, then I will make a cup of tea and have three pieces of dark chocolate.
- If I want to give up on my run, then I will walk for five minutes and then resume running.

- If there are stairs, then I will always take them.

Now it's your turn!

TAKE IT TO THE NEXT LEVEL

Create an if/then plan for the different impulses you're likely to encounter on your path to a certain goal. Use your plan when those obstacles present themselves. You can write your plan in the space here, or in a separate notebook.

_____

_____

_____

_____

_____

_____

_____

_____

_____

_____

_____

_____

_____

_____

_____

_____

EXERCISE 47:
SET INTERNAL BOUNDARIES

Earlier in this chapter, the "Establish Boundaries" exercise outlines the importance of setting boundaries with others. In contrast, *internal* boundaries are between you and you! They're the limits or rules you establish for yourself that help regulate your emotions, manage your time effectively, and maintain control over your impulses.

This type of self-discipline is a critical aspect of success. Some people look at others achieving their goals and think that they must have superhuman willpower. Rest assured, that's not a thing! Even the toughest people have strong impulses—but they have even stronger commitments with themselves. Knowing how many cookies you can eat, how much time you must spend working out, what portion of your paycheck you can spend on yourself each month—these are all examples of internal boundaries. Abiding by these rules can keep you on track and provide much-needed balance in your life.

By exerting self-control in small, even seemingly insignificant moments, you'll begin to form a pattern of choosing to honor yourself over choosing what's immediately gratifying. It's not only essential for a balanced life—it's essential for leveling up.

Internal boundaries don't always need to involve something external, like cookies or the gym. Some of the most important boundaries you can set with yourself are centered on managing your thoughts and emotions—how you speak to yourself, how you cope with emotions, and being accountable for how you treat others.

TAKE IT TO THE NEXT LEVEL

Create your own set of internal boundaries that will support and empower you to achieve your goals. Keep two things in mind:

1. Make them very specific. Vague boundaries leave room for confusion...and excuses. For example, say your boundary involves saying no to more things so you can have more time for your kids. Without knowing the parameters of when or what you're supposed to say no to, you might only realize that you haven't honored your boundaries after the fact.
2. Communicate your internal boundaries as needed. The people in your life are not mind readers. If you want them to respect the boundaries you've made for yourself, make them known! Similar to external boundaries, most people will be willing to respect them if they're aware they exist.

EXERCISE 48:
ASK "WHY?" FIVE TIMES

Do you ever stop to ask yourself why you're getting so impatient? The unwillingness to wait for someone or something always warrants the question, "Why?" If you're noticing a pattern with your impatience—such as always giving up on your goals, or constantly yelling at your spouse or child—it could be posing a bigger problem in your life. And what's the best way to solve a problem? Get to the root of it!

TAKE IT TO THE NEXT LEVEL

You can complete this exercise with hindsight, using past experience, or you can use it the next time your patience is being tested. Actually, why not do both? Give it a try now using a past experience—then you'll know exactly how to use it in the moment.

1. Ask yourself why you think you're getting so impatient.
2. If your answer doesn't identify the root cause, then ask again.
3. Then ask again—and again.
4. By the time you've asked "Why?" five times, you will have uncovered other information that might lead you to respond to the situation in a different way.

Keep in mind that you might need to ask "Why?" fewer or more than five times. Stop when you've identified the root cause of your impatience.

Here's an example of the technique in practice:

1. "Why do I always get so impatient with my kids in the morning and start my day off on the wrong foot?" Because our mornings are so chaotic.
2. "Why are mornings so chaotic?" Because the kids don't wake up on time, they never have their backpacks ready, and I'm rushing to figure out what to make for breakfast.
3. "Why am I always rushing?" Because I don't make sure everything is prepared the night before.

4. "Why don't I make sure everything is prepared the night before?" Because after dinner, all I want to do is relax on the couch and watch TV.
5. "Why?"

The final answer here could be one of many, which would result in very different solutions. The other thing to note is that the root of the problem appears to be coming from the parent, not the children. Use the five whys technique to take ownership of your impatience and make a change!

CHAPTER 6

EXERCISES TO INCREASE OPTIMISM

Do you see the glass as half full or half empty? If your answer is half empty, this chapter is especially for you! People who see the glass as half empty are more likely to magnify problems in their own minds and seek out evidence for the least favorable outcomes. Assuming that the worst will happen, they take a pessimistic view of the world. On the flip side, optimists have more positive expectations for life and don't take to heart every thought that occurs to them. Interestingly, this positive attitude is what separates mental toughness from simple resilience. While a resilient person can bounce back from hardships, a mentally tough person will do so with a hopeful outlook that enables them to keep working toward their goals no matter the setbacks or uncertainties.

If optimism isn't your natural state, don't worry. It's teachable! In the following exercises, you will cultivate a more optimistic perspective by learning to see things as clearly and accurately as possible. It's about cultivating not just positive thinking but also "nonnegative" thinking. It's not always easy to maintain optimism, but with dedicated effort and practice, you can begin to see the glass as half full and approach hardship in a more productive way.

EXERCISE 49:
REFRAME NEGATIVE THOUGHTS

Wouldn't it be cool if you could catch your irrational thoughts before they spiraled out of control and impacted your behavior? It's totally possible with a little patience, awareness, and determined effort. Reframing is a technique you can use to catch an untrue thought while you're having it and replace it with a more objective one. By changing your perspective, you consequently change the way you feel and behave. Essential to building mental strength—and the first step in learning to reframe a situation—is identifying your negative automatic thoughts. These are subconscious, negatively framed interpretations you have about yourself, the world around you, and how you think the future will unfold. These thoughts, or "frames," are based on long-held beliefs that are self-defeating and illogical and that tend to have a damaging effect on your mood and behavior. To level up on optimism, identify your common negative automatic thoughts and find alternative positive thoughts for each.

TAKE IT TO THE NEXT LEVEL

Writing negative automatic thoughts out on paper can help you highlight patterns of thinking and make it easier to challenge them. Make a list of the unhelpful, automatic thoughts that keep coming back to you—the ones that upset you the most and cause the strongest emotional reaction. If you're not sure where to start, think about unhealthy thinking patterns surrounding perfection, guilt, blame, comparison, all-or-nothing thinking, or mind reading (presuming to know what other people are thinking without looking at the evidence). Here are some examples of negative automatic thoughts:

- I'm not smart enough
- I'm a bad mother
- I'm going to lose my job
- My friend hates me
- I'm not attractive enough
- I'm a failure

One by one, go through each of the thoughts you identified and look at the evidence for and against the thought. Question the source of it and come to a realistic assessment of the situation. If you need help, ponder the following questions:

- How helpful is this way of thinking?
- Is there something I'm not seeing or something I'm ignoring?
- What would a friend say about this thought?
- Is there a deep belief or fear driving this thought?
- Is there a more realistic way to think?

Here's an example:

1. Thought: My friend hates me.
2. Evidence: We got into a fight, but I know she loves me, and we've gotten into fights before without it hurting our friendship. She never said she hated me—it's a fear I have because of a friendship I lost many years ago.

Now find a more helpful, constructive interpretation of each thought, creating a more balanced way of thinking. Here is a way to reframe the previous example:

1. Thought: My friend hates me.
2. Reframe: My friend and I have some issues to work through, but we'll probably bounce back even stronger in the end.

Now that you're more aware of these tendencies, practice reframing your negative automatic thoughts every chance you can.

EXERCISE 50: USE POSITIVE AFFIRMATIONS

Negative beliefs about yourself can become self-fulfilling prophecies. Think about it: When was the last time your internal self-talk told you that you weren't good enough at something or that you were sure to fail? What was the result? It's likely that your mood and confidence took a hit and subsequently undermined the outcome.

Positive affirmations do just the opposite! They encourage an optimistic mindset and help program your brain to believe whatever positive mental repetitions you're feeding it. These brief, encouraging statements have the power to drive true change and set you up for success. You can use affirmations that have been created by others or you can create your own statements perfectly tailored to suit your needs. One thing is for sure: Positive affirmations work best when they're repeated often to combat their opposing, self-limiting belief.

TAKE IT TO THE NEXT LEVEL

Make a list of your perceived negative qualities that play on repeat in your mind. Include any core beliefs that you developed as a result of other people's criticism or that may be creating a self-fulfilling prophecy.

Once you have your list, create an affirmation that is the opposite of each self-judgment. Your affirmations should be positive and motivating. Make them one or two sentences each, using first person and present tense. Here are some examples of negative thoughts and corresponding affirmations:

Thought: I'm not good enough.
Affirmation: I accept and love the person I am and who I am becoming.

Thought: I can't handle stress.
Affirmation: I will use the tools at my disposal, and I will get through this!

Thought: I'm too old for _____.
Affirmation: Now is the perfect time to go after my dreams. I have more knowledge and experience now than I ever have before.

Thought: I'm not good with money.
Affirmation: Money flows freely to me. I can look at my finances without fear.

After you've created your affirmations, start putting them into practice! You're now prepared with a rebuttal for each of your most detrimental self-beliefs. Commit to stopping these negative thoughts in their tracks and silencing them with encouraging affirmations. You can recite them in your head, write them down, or say them out loud. Just make sure you repeat them over and over and with conviction. Bonus tip: In time, you may be able to recognize in advance when negative thoughts will be triggered. Then you can use affirmations proactively.

EXERCISE 51: SUBTRACT NEGATIVITY

Scientific research proves that negativity is contagious! Negative messages rely on your psychological fear response, which in turn causes you to pay more attention to them.

Optimism, on the other hand, can take more effort. In order to maintain an optimistic outlook, you not only have to do the internal work but also consider your environment. Your surroundings influence your experience to a large degree, and this includes your mindset. Environment includes the spaces and conditions that you live and work in, as well as your relationships and interactions with others. Is your living space organized and decorated in ways that inspire contentment and revitalization? Or is it cluttered and adding to your stress level? Do you surround yourself with people who look for silver linings and see the glass as half full? Or are you more often listening to complaints and drama?

To increase optimism in your life, try eliminating some unnecessary negativity from your environment. What can you subtract that would ultimately increase positivity?

TAKE IT TO THE NEXT LEVEL

The following is a broad list of things you might want to consider eliminating, limiting, or taking a break from in order to increase optimism in your life. Go through the list and get real with yourself. Where is negativity breeding, and what can you do to minimize it?

- Toxic/negative relationships (people who make you feel bad about yourself and/or tend to drain your energy)
- Drama
- Harmful distractions
- Unproductive habits
- Negative content (e.g., social media accounts)
- Clutter
- Anything else that you don't want in your life because it's bringing you down

Just remember: When things aren't adding up in your life, start subtracting!

EXERCISE 52:
LOOK FOR SILVER LININGS

A key component of optimism is being able to see the bright side when things go wrong. When an optimist faces adversity, they don't dwell on the negative aspects of what's happened—they instead find a way to appreciate the experience. How do you make sense of the negative events that occur in your own life? A positive outlook will enable you to push through with confidence and bounce back even stronger than you were before.

Realistically, there's almost always something to be grateful for in every situation. If you miss out on one opportunity, you'll be available when the next opportunity comes around—and it might even be a better one! If you get in an argument with someone, there may be something to learn from it about communication, the relationship, or yourself. Whether or not you see the silver lining in a situation is within your control.

TAKE IT TO THE NEXT LEVEL

Get yourself in a positive state of mind by closing your eyes and conjuring up happy memories. Once you have your images, open your eyes and grab your notebook to complete this exercise:

1. Think about a recent time that you felt frustrated, upset, or defeated because something didn't go your way. Briefly describe it in writing.
2. List as many silver linings as you can possibly think of for that situation. At a minimum, try to come up with three

positive things that resulted or are likely to result from that experience.

3. Repeat steps 1 to 3 a few more times, recalling recent negative events and brainstorming silver linings.

Remember to utilize this exercise the next time you're faced with a disappointment. Over time, you will instinctively look for the silver linings when things don't go your way.

EXERCISE 53: CULTIVATE GRATITUDE AND SET YOUR INTENTIONS

It turns out that "waking up on the wrong side of the bed" is a real thing! Research has shown that people who wake up expecting to have a stressful day can actually impair their mental abilities and performance—even if the anticipated stress never actually occurs. If success is what you're after, it's best to start your day with an optimistic outlook and focus on how you *do* want things to unfold. It's all about your perspective.

So before your feet even touch the floor each morning, consider how you want your day to go, and bring to mind all the amazing things this life has to offer you. Cultivate gratitude and expect good things to happen.

TAKE IT TO THE NEXT LEVEL

It's time to get up on the right side of the bed. As soon as you wake up in the morning, grab your notebook and write down at least three things that you're grateful for. These can be as small as your warm bed or linen sheets or as big as your loving partner or your interesting job. Try not to repeat any item from one morning to the next. Then write down three positive intentions for your day ahead. This isn't a to-do list but rather a list of how you would like the day to go and what you would like to bring to the world. For example, your intentions could be to practice being present, to be as productive as possible, and to do something nice for someone. Give this exercise a try for an entire week and see how you feel.

EXERCISE 54:
ENVISION YOUR BEST FUTURE

Optimism plays a big role in fostering mental toughness. Why? Because building optimism about the future can motivate you to actually work toward that desired future, making it more likely to become a reality!

What does your best, happiest, most fulfilling future look like? Consider the different areas of your life: career, family, health, social situations, and so on. What would each of these areas look like if you achieved all your goals? Envision this scenario with all of its sights, sounds—even tastes and smells! This practice not only promotes optimism; it can also illuminate what you want out of life and get you thinking about your priorities and what you need to do to reach your goals.

TAKE IT TO THE NEXT LEVEL

Start writing about that best possible future in detail! The more specific, the better. Imagine what your day-to-day would look like, what you would be doing for work, how you would feel, etc. Steer clear of unproductive thoughts, such as barriers to being able to bring this future to fruition, or reasons why you've failed in the past. These thoughts are irrelevant to this exercise. Only focus on the brightest future, where you're your absolute best self!

Recall this best future scenario anytime you need a boost of optimism. When you're feeling unclear about your goals or low on motivation, come back to this vision of your future and allow it to steer you in the right direction.

EXERCISE 55: THINK ABUNDANTLY

When you're feeling stuck or getting less than amazing results in an aspect of your life, it can be helpful to identify your mindset. Are you making decisions based on fear? Do you often feel like you're not good enough or there's not enough to go around? Are you so focused on never failing that you forget to embrace uncertainty and open your mind to possibility? If this sounds familiar, you may be operating from a scarcity mindset. By comparison, an abundance mindset operates from a deep sense of personal worth and security, and the belief that there are more than enough resources and success for everyone.

While the human instinct to think with a scarcity mindset may be a mechanism to protect yourself from anything deemed a threat, it's often based on self-limiting beliefs, not facts. Just because you didn't succeed at something once doesn't mean you'll "never be good enough at anything." Just because you don't have a lot of money now doesn't mean you'll "always be broke."

Your mindset can drastically affect your performance at nearly every level. If you believe something is not in the realm of possibility, you'll be scared to even try—or may give it less than your best effort. And if you believe there's "not enough," you'll be so focused on keeping what you have that you won't seek out new opportunities.

TAKE IT TO THE NEXT LEVEL

From the following list, see if you identify with any of these common toxic beliefs that come from a scarcity mindset. Keep in mind that these are generalizations:

- I'm not _____ enough to go after what I want
- I don't deserve it
- The system/others have put me at a disadvantage
- The future is going to be bad because things aren't so good right now
- There's not enough success to go around

Now, using the following example for guidance, re-create any of the scarcity stories that are affecting your life currently or have done so in the past. Then reframe the story to see how much more likely you'd be to succeed with an abundance mindset.

You get an email from a recruiter informing you that you didn't get the job you were interviewing for. You then proceed through this scarcity loop:

- Scarcity Mindset: "I'm not smart enough. I'll never find a new job."
- Poor Choice: You stop applying for jobs because what's the use?
- Negative Outcome: You stay stuck in a job you hate.

Here's the same situation, reframed with an abundance mentality:

- Abundance Mindset: "That wasn't the right fit for me. My dream job is still out there!"
- Wise Choice: You keep applying to jobs and continue along the process.
- Positive Outcome: You eventually get a job you love.

EXERCISE 56:
CULTIVATE CONTENTMENT

Notice how this exercise is not called "Cultivate Happiness." This is because happiness is a fleeting state, and whatever you currently think is going to make you happy might not be all that great once you achieve it. The pursuit of happiness might make you miss out on a lot of important stuff along the way from point A (your present circumstances) to point B (said happiness that you're chasing).

Surely there must be something good happening between point A and point B?

So how can you appreciate the goal striving and not just the goal attainment? The answer lies in contentment. Contentment is the feeling of being satisfied and at peace with your current circumstances. It's a conscious decision to be happy with what you already have. It's being able to say, "Yes, I'm striving for x, y, and z, but life is already great as it stands. I'm working through my flaws, but I'm already a complete, amazing individual." Being content means accepting that negative emotions are part of the human experience—knowing that while it's great to be able to work through and improve negative emotional states, it's okay to feel down, anxious, or scared at times. This type of radical acceptance is the key to reducing how much you will suffer when times are hard, and it also provides you the mental resources to shift into a more positive space.

It's important to keep in mind that contentment is not feeling like everything needs to be exactly as you wish it to be in order to be happy. This idea that happiness is contingent upon some external factor just doesn't hold up. Success doesn't fuel happiness; happiness fuels success! Research has shown time and time again that winners are not happier than losers. Upon winning, they may feel a great sense of accomplishment, but eventually, they'll return to the same baseline of happiness as before the major achievement. So instead of striving for happiness, why not aim for contentment? Shed the expectations of how you think life ought to be. Aim for improvements, but maintain gratitude and acceptance throughout.

TAKE IT TO THE NEXT LEVEL

For this exercise you're going to identify any well-being contingencies you might have—the things you're depending on to bring you happiness. Write them down in your notebook and reflect on them.

For guidance, take a look at these examples of well-being contingencies:

- When I find my life partner, then I'll be happy
- When I reach that career milestone, then I'll finally enjoy my job
- When I have x amount of money in my bank account, then I can enjoy life
- When I purchase x, then I'll be happy
- When I get validation from x, then I'll be satisfied
- When I accomplish x, then I'll feel fulfilled

When you see your expectations written out like this, it becomes clear how silly it is to live this way. They might take a whole lifetime to fulfill, and there's no guarantee that they ever even will! Does that mean you'll never be happy? No! Think about how you can take ownership of your well-being and learn to love your life as it already is.

EXERCISE 57:
END DOOMSCROLLING

There's a limitless amount of content online that we could get lost in for hours on end—and that's exactly what's happening! But more often than not, we get lost in the negative stuff. There's a growing body of evidence that humans prioritize negative news over positive news. After all, bad news is typically what dominates the headlines. Studies also show that negative content is more likely to be perceived as truthful.

There's a new term that refers to the tendency to get lost in negative content: *Doomscrolling* is continuously scrolling through bad news, consuming article after article, video after video. We can't seem to look away.

But there's a not-so-fine line between staying informed and staying fixated on what is wrong with the world. Being an optimist doesn't mean that you don't recognize life's challenges. It means that despite those challenges, you choose to focus on what is good, because focusing on the negative is not very productive. Simply put, the difference between an optimist and a pessimist is what you choose to focus on. You are in control of your negative-content consumption!

TAKE IT TO THE NEXT LEVEL

In this exercise, you will track and then limit your negative news consumption for one week.

1. For the first three days, use a stopwatch to keep track of online sessions that include any sort of negative content.

Determine the average number of minutes spent each day (total minutes ÷ 3 = average minutes per day).

2. For the next four days, use a timer to stop yourself once you've reached half of your average time from the first three days. For example, if you spent an average of thirty minutes per day on negative consumption during the first part of the week, you can now only spend fifteen minutes per day consuming negative news.

3. At the end of the week, reflect on this exercise. Do you see the value in placing limitations on yourself? Do you still feel informed? Do you generally feel more positive?

What you choose to do with your insights is up to you, but at the very least, try to balance the depressing stuff with some positive, uplifting content.

EXERCISE 58:
RECOGNIZE DISTORTED THINKING

Do you trust your brain to make the best decisions for you? It turns out that as powerful as that mighty brain of yours is, it does have its limitations. While it's generally reliable, on some occasions you may want to second-guess what it's telling you.

When your brain is attempting to process, interpret, and simplify information, it has a tendency to make connections where there aren't any. These cognitive distortions help your brain reach decisions as quickly and efficiently as possible. But they often misrepresent reality and influence the way you make sense of the world around you.

It's important to have a general understanding of these biases because—to put it bluntly—sometimes your brain lies to you! And this means that sometimes optimism requires that you challenge your mind's default pessimism. Here are some of the most common biases:

1. Confirmation bias: When you favor information that conforms to your existing beliefs and discount evidence that does not conform.
2. Self-serving bias: The tendency to blame external forces when bad things happen and to give yourself credit when good things happen.
3. Hindsight bias: When you become convinced that you predicted an outcome beforehand, leading to the conclusion that you can predict other outcomes.
4. Actor-observer bias: The tendency to attribute your own actions to external causes, while attributing other people's actions to internal causes.
5. Anchoring bias: The tendency to rely too heavily on the very first piece of information learned.
6. Attentional bias: The tendency to pay attention to some things while simultaneously ignoring others.
7. Availability heuristic bias: The tendency to place greater value on information that comes to mind quickly and using that information to predict future events.

TAKE IT TO THE NEXT LEVEL

Follow these steps to examine where your own thinking may be distorted:

1. Go through each of the distortions previously listed. Make sure you understand each of them.
2. Once you have a grasp on what each of these biases means and how they impact your decisions, try to come up with at least one example of how each one has negatively distorted your thinking in the past.
3. Do you notice any patterns? Do you have tendencies toward some biases more than others?

Things aren't always what they seem. When you find yourself assuming the worst, think back to this exercise and the tendencies you have toward certain distortions. Consider how these factors influence your decisions and challenge them.

EXERCISE 59:
PRACTICE TWENTY-FOUR HOURS OF JOY

It's a tough world out there; sometimes it's all you can do to keep your head above water. Career, family, and social obligations can be demanding, often leaving you with little energy left at the end of the day.

Through times of stress and hardship, focusing on the little things can go a long way in shifting your mindset and energy. Things like the shining moon and stars; the beautiful sunrise;

warm, freshly laundered sheets on your bed; or a family dinner can quickly add up, building up your sense of optimism.

TAKE IT TO THE NEXT LEVEL

Where can you find more joy in your life today? For the next twenty-four hours, commit yourself to finding joy in the simple pleasures of life. Seek out the goodness as opposed to focusing on the negative.

EXERCISE 60: MAKE A POSITIVE CONTRIBUTION

Optimists make a habit of donating their time and energy to a cause greater than themselves. Whether it be giving back to their communities or being available to people they know, they understand the value of contribution. It not only helps others, but giving back can also put things into perspective, making you feel more positive about your own circumstances. Just think about the last time you did something good for someone else out of the kindness of your heart. How did it make you feel? Research shows that performing acts of kindness boosts your mood and ultimately makes you more optimistic and positive!

TAKE IT TO THE NEXT LEVEL

If you're able to commit a decent amount of time and effort, consider a formal volunteering program, but know that this isn't the only way you can make a difference. Friends, family, and coworkers may benefit from your time as well. All contributions are valuable, and all people have a way of contributing!

How do you feel you can best volunteer your time? Is there a cause you already feel strongly about? Can you offer a specific skill set? Consider your availability and schedule, and then decide if and how you can be of service to others moving forward.

CHAPTER 7

EXERCISES TO CONFRONT STRESS

Stress narrows your ability to think clearly and function effectively. It can manifest in times of uncertainty or when you're facing big changes, overwhelming responsibilities, or relationship conflicts. And it's unavoidable. You can certainly do everything within your control to prevent the mental or emotional strain that comes from such circumstances, but some stressors are inevitable. The best way to overcome stress is to accept that it's a part of life and be prepared to manage it effectively. Unfortunately, habitual responses to stress are often unhealthy and do more harm than good. This might include bingeing on TV, food, or alcohol, withdrawing from friends, or lashing out at others. Everyone's reaction is different. Knowing your particular tendencies and developing healthier, alternative responses to stress are important parts of improving your overall mental toughness. Knowing your triggers—things that typically cause you stress—is another key step.

In this chapter you'll figure out what your tendencies are when you're stressed and begin to replace unhealthy coping mechanisms with healthier ones. You'll also develop a customized self-care plan to prevent stress and use conscious breathing and positive anchors to bring you into a calmer, more focused state of mind when the going gets tough.

EXERCISE 61:
FIND YOUR CENTER

When you're centered, there's no resistance—you're living in the moment, alert, calm, connected, balanced, and neutral (not positive or negative, just existing). Though there are physical regions associated with your center, for example your heart or stomach, it doesn't have an exact location. It's more like an energetic reference point to come back to when life's challenges have pushed you off-balance.

It's extremely helpful to find your center before delivering a speech, having a difficult conversation, or any number of stressful activities, in order to remain calm and collected—and more likely to succeed. So what does it look like to be off-center? Here are some common indicators:

- Being easily distracted, unable to focus
- Reactivity
- Laziness and procrastination
- Negative self-talk
- Feeling overwhelmed, scattered, and high-strung
- Feeling lost
- Struggling with impulse control
- Feeling fatigued early in the day
- Going to bed really late or really early

Recognizing these signs and knowing how to bring yourself back to a state of equilibrium are valuable coping skills and key to being mentally tough.

TAKE IT TO THE NEXT LEVEL

Try the following centering exercise and make it a regular practice anytime you are feeling unbalanced, need to improve your focus, or manage stress. The more you practice, the easier it will be to center yourself.

1. Lie on your back on a comfortable surface. Sitting or standing is fine too.
2. If lying down or sitting, plant your feet on the floor with your knees bent.
3. Close your mouth and take slow, deep, rhythmic breaths through your nose, originating from your belly. Try to make your exhales longer than your inhales.
4. As you gradually begin to feel more calm, try to inhale and exhale for longer periods.
5. Continue breathing this way for a few minutes. Notice any physical and mental changes that have taken place, and remember this feeling for next time.

EXERCISE 62: ESTABLISH HEALTHY COPING STRATEGIES

A key part of mental toughness is dealing effectively with stress and performing to the best of your abilities, regardless of the circumstances. That sounds like a tall order! How are you supposed to be calm when things seem to be falling apart?

It's about healthy coping. When negative events occur, coping strategies can help you tolerate or distract from them in a safe way. There are two main types of healthy, adaptive coping responses that help you feel better in the moment without hurting yourself or anyone else:

1. Problem-solving strategies
2. Emotion-focused strategies

A problem-solving strategy is typically triggered by stress that's perceived to be changeable (e.g., challenges at work), and it focuses on tackling the issue in order to reduce stress. An emotion-focused strategy is used more in unchangeable situations (e.g., the death of a loved one) to nurture your emotional well-being during the stressful time. Some examples of problem-solving strategies include:

* Asking others for help
* Distancing or removing yourself from the source of stress
* Making a to-do list or action plan
* Practicing better time management
* Evaluating the pros and cons of a particular decision

Here are some examples of emotion-focused strategies:

* Spending time in nature
* Creative activities such as writing, drawing, or playing an instrument
* Calling or visiting a loved one
* Reframing the situation (see the "Reframe Negative Thoughts" exercise in Chapter 6)

- Practicing deep breathing, yoga, or meditation
- Seeking counseling

Can your current stress be eased more by problem-solving strategies or emotion-focused strategies?

TAKE IT TO THE NEXT LEVEL

Follow these steps to establish coping mechanisms that work best for you:

1. Go through the previous lists of strategies and circle any that you're instinctively drawn to within each type.
2. Now brainstorm as many more as you can for each coping type.
3. Write down all your chosen strategies in your notebook. This is your go-to list for coping with a stressful situation!

The next time you're confronted with stress, try one or more of these strategies and learn what helps you to de-stress. Experts say you may need to alternate between several strategies to cope with a stressful event most effectively.

EXERCISE 63:
ASK, "WHAT'S THE WORST THAT COULD HAPPEN?"

Have you ever reacted emotionally to something that never ended up happening? Sure, the worst-case scenario may occur, but how likely is that? Many of the things you spend so much time stressing about will never actually come to pass. When it comes to building mental strength and crushing your goals, this habit is nothing but a waste of time and energy!

Stepping back and viewing the situation for what it is can make it feel more manageable and kick your brain into problem-solving mode. You can also rehearse your response to what may happen, restoring confidence in your abilities, and feeling better prepared to face what does happen. You may even come to realize that your problem is not as bad as you thought.

TAKE IT TO THE NEXT LEVEL

In this exercise you'll label the fears that are causing you stress and shrink them down to size.

1. Think of a situation in your life that brings up feelings of fear and anticipatory anxiety.
2. Now imagine the worst possible negative consequence that could happen—within reason! Be realistic; rehearse it and make it as real as possible.
3. Plan how you would respond if this were to actually happen. How would you mitigate the situation? How would you cope?

4. Accept this scenario as a possibility and then release it with gratitude, knowing that at the very least it will teach you something. You will also be ready for it should it happen.

After you've completed this activity, throw any thoughts about this worst-case scenario out the window and focus on the most positive and desirable outcome. The aim is to realize that you can handle any situation with some effort and planning.

EXERCISE 64: KNOW YOUR STRESS RESPONSE

Everyone reacts differently to stressful situations. How do you typically respond? Over time, you've undoubtedly developed your own unique ways of coping with big changes, negative events, and difficult emotions. These coping strategies involve some combination of behaviors, thoughts, and emotions that help you adjust to stressful situations. They're the specific activities you engage in to maintain your mental health and well-being during times of distress.

It's important to recognize, though, that some coping strategies are more helpful than others. A mentally strong individual will adapt to stress in healthy and effective ways, steering clear of coping methods that can be counterproductive. While positive coping strategies aim to keep you present and actively working toward solving your problems, maladaptive strategies often provide instant relief but have unintended consequences in the long run. Here are some examples of unhealthy coping strategies:

* Excessive drinking
* Criticizing yourself
* Avoiding friends and family
* Chewing your fingernails
* Eating too much or too little

Like many mental habits, maladaptive coping strategies are usually carried out unconsciously and often developed early in life—making them ingrained behaviors that can be challenging to transform. You developed these coping responses because they helped you survive and were effective at one point in time, but they're not anymore. Why? Because you're in the process of leveling up! This requires finding effective methods for managing your stress, as opposed to quick-fix solutions that favor immediate gratification over long-term success.

TAKE IT TO THE NEXT LEVEL

1. What kinds of behaviors make you feel better when you're distressed? Make a list of them. This list may or may not contain some of the strategies listed earlier. For examples of healthy coping strategies, check out the "Establish Healthy Coping Strategies" exercise in this chapter.
2. While some of your behaviors may genuinely benefit you, some of them may be more harmful than helpful—even the ones that you think aren't so bad. Go through the list

and try to see what potential downsides there might be for each one. How does each one *not* work for you?

3. For each of the behaviors that have negative consequences, try to come up with a healthy alternative.

While it may be easy enough to pick some healthy alternatives and write them down, the difficulty will be putting them into practice. Now that you're aware of your automatic responses to stress, try to use this information to guide you through the next challenging situation you're faced with. Think about how effective your usual response is in the long run, even if it makes you feel good in the moment. These are the pivotal opportunities to exercise your budding mental muscles!

EXERCISE 65: CUSTOMIZE A SELF-CARE ROUTINE

There's a softer side of mental toughness, and it involves knowing when and how to take care of yourself. How can you expect to bounce back stronger after crises if you're feeling physically and emotionally depleted? When you're feeling your best, your body is primed to confront stress and be more resilient.

Self-care is the regular practice of prioritizing your well-being in a way that meets your specific needs. Generally, your self-care will fall under the categories of physical (acts of care for your body, e.g., drinking plenty of water and eating well), emotional (acts of care that help you release negative feelings and encourage positive feelings, e.g., writing in a journal and talking with a therapist), and mental (acts of care that strengthen your mind and recenter your thoughts, e.g., learning something new and meditating). It's essential to take care of yourself when you recognize signs of stress, but prioritizing your wellness regularly is an important preventative measure as well. Regular self-care can enhance the likelihood of successful coping later.

TAKE IT TO THE NEXT LEVEL

A self-care strategy is not one-size-fits-all. Go through the following acts of care and pick out things that you feel would work well in terms of relaxing, soothing, nurturing, or centering yourself.

Physical self-care:
- Get a massage
- Exercise
- Cook a nourishing meal
- Take a warm bath
- Get a good night's sleep

Emotional self-care:
- Volunteer for a meaningful cause
- Make a gratitude list
- Hang out with loved ones
- Spend time in nature
- Express yourself through drawing, painting, or coloring

Mental self-care:
- Meditate
- Play a board game

- Read a good book
- Work on a hobby you enjoy
- Take a trip somewhere new

Start filling out this list even more with your own ideas. Be sure you have a number of options listed under each of the three categories. If you are unsure of where to start or what to include, consider what kinds of self-supporting activities are currently missing from your life. Some people need to prioritize alone time because they're always around others, while others will need to work social activities into their routine for the opposite reason. Your customized self-care plan may include lots of physical activity if you sit at a desk through your entire workday. Or perhaps you're always on your feet, and massages and baths sound like a dream. Determine your personal needs for having a more balanced, healthy life.

Once you've got an idea of the activities that suit your needs best, work some of them into your routine for the next week. Make a point to block off time for these activities and get in the routine of taking care of your well-being! After the week is through, notice how you feel. Chances are you'll feel more refreshed and eager to schedule your self-care for the following week and beyond.

EXERCISE 66:
TRY THE COLD-WATER CHALLENGE

People who are mentally tough are primed to take on stress. They challenge themselves consistently because they know that good things happen outside of their comfort zone. With practice, you too can train your brain to know that whatever happens, you've got things under control!

This cold-shock exercise is based on an ancient Ayurvedic remedy known as cold therapy, which was popularized by Wim Hof, a.k.a. "the Iceman"—a man whose name is synonymous with mental toughness. The cold-water challenge works by triggering the sympathetic nervous system, increasing blood flow to the brain, and reducing stress levels (as well as promoting positive hormonal changes that affect mood, focus, and attention).

Cold-shocking the body is both a natural stress reliever and a powerful mindset challenge that lets you practice breathing through stressful situations. As you persevere and push past your limits day after day, you will learn that stress is merely what your mind makes of it, and that you can get through anything!

Just be sure to talk to your doctor before trying this challenge, as it may not be suitable for some, especially those with certain health conditions.

TAKE IT TO THE NEXT LEVEL

Cold-water exposure is most beneficial when performed first thing in the morning, but feel free to make adjustments based on your needs and circumstances. The important thing is that you take the plunge.

1. At the end of your daily shower, prepare yourself for what's to come. Get hyped! Tell yourself you love cold showers. You're excited to start the day by accomplishing what many would consider an impossible task.
2. Take several deep and steady breaths, and when you're ready, turn the tap all the way to cold. Ideally you want to aim for about 68°F, but if you don't have a thermometer, just shoot for ice cold.
3. Submerge your whole body under the water—especially your head. Your body's initial reaction will cause your breath to become short and shallow, but concentrating on your breathing will help to distract you, as well as calm you down. Refocus your attention and try for slow, deep breaths.
4. Continue the cold exposure for anywhere from ten seconds to a couple of minutes. If you're new to this challenge, consider starting with ten seconds and increasing the time every day. If ten seconds is not doable at first, even a brief burst of cold water is a great start.

After the initial shock of the experience, most people report feeling highly energized, focused, and awake. Enjoy the benefits of stepping up to such an intense challenge. Keep up with this practice for as long as you see fit but try to commit to at least one week of cold-water immersion. The degree to which you commit to pushing past your comfort zone is up to you and only you.

EXERCISE 67:
BEFRIEND UNCERTAINTY

You go to an interview in the hope of getting a job. You study for an exam in the hope of getting a good grade. You go on a date in the hope of finding love. In all of these scenarios, you invest your time in the present in order to possibly achieve something in the future. There's a real sense of vulnerability in the space between your efforts and the desired outcome. What if I answered those interview questions wrong? What if I fail my course? What if my date doesn't like me?

This vulnerability about the uncertain future can cause a great deal of stress and anxiety. As such, you may find yourself engaging in certain behaviors to try to remove or avoid that uncertainty—things like overanalyzing, seeking reassurance from others, or trying to solve an unsolvable problem. These behaviors require a lot of time and energy that could be spent on more meaningful and productive tasks.

People vary in their ability to tolerate uncertainty, but you can guess where the mentally tough ones fall on that scale! Tolerance for uncertainty is a key component of a strong and resilient mindset. If you can learn to let go of what you can't control, you can save yourself from a lot of unnecessary stress, freeing up your mental energy to better handle your circumstances.

TAKE IT TO THE NEXT LEVEL

The more intolerant you are of uncertainty, the stronger your reaction to it. This exercise will help you build your tolerance and accept that life will always have unpredictable moments. The following is a chart for exploring how you handle uncertainty. Use it as a template to create your own chart in your notebook, then use the following steps to fill it out:

THINGS I DO TO REDUCE UNCERTAINTY	ANXIETY LEVEL (1–10)	NOTES
Seek excessive reassurance or advice		
Overthink or overanalyze mundane decisions		
Keep myself constantly busy or distracted		
Procrastinate or avoid certain people, places, or things		
Constantly check up on someone or something		

1. What kinds of things do you normally do to try to avoid or reduce feelings of uncertainty? List your common behaviors in your chart.
2. Imagine how anxious you would become if you could not engage in each behavior. Rank each one on a scale from 1 to 10—1 being no anxiety at all, 10 being extremely anxious.

3. In your day-to-day life, practice behaving as though you're more comfortable with uncertainty by not engaging in these behaviors. Start small with the less difficult behaviors (1) and work your way up to greater difficulty (10).

4. In the Notes section of your chart, keep track of how the previous step went. What did you do differently? How did you feel? Was it easier or harder than you thought? Did things turn out okay, even if you weren't 100 percent certain? If things didn't turn out okay, what happened? How did you cope? What does this tell you about your ability to cope with negative outcomes in the future?

There's no timeline for this activity. Just start by becoming aware of how you act and creating your chart. When you see opportunities to build your tolerance for uncertainty, seize them. As you keep practicing, it will become easier to accept uncertainty as a part of life.

EXERCISE 68: SCHEDULE TIME TO WORRY

You might have read the title of this exercise and thought, "What the heck?" It may seem odd at first, but think about it: Would you rather spend all day in a state of stress and anxiety, or find a way to contain it to just twenty or thirty minutes?

By its very nature, worry lives in the past and in the future, making it impossible to stay in the present moment. And this inability to stay present can impair your focus, performance, relationships, and more. Since worrying does little more than consume your mental energy, put a limit on it! Mentally tough people are known to set aside time to think through any issues that may be weighing on their minds. During this dedicated time, they can worry as much as they want. Once their worry time is up, they move forward, ready to thrive in the present. This proven method can work especially well for natural worriers, who always have their fingers on the pulse of what might go wrong, or for those times when something specific is stressing you out.

TAKE IT TO THE NEXT LEVEL

Research has shown that this strategy can provide anxiety relief within about two weeks! So for the next fourteen days, find a twenty-minute time slot in your day (or thirty minutes, depending on your needs) and devote it to worrying. During this time, you can write out your stress, try to come up with solutions, or simply just worry. But when the timer is up, that's it! When your mind slips into worry mode, gently remind yourself that there is a specific time for worrying and this is not it. With practice, this will get easier, and hopefully you'll find that you're no longer being consumed by your worries at all hours.

Bonus tip: Do not schedule your worry time too close to when you go to sleep.

EXERCISE 69:
LEARN TO SAY NO

One of the keys to managing stress is to control your time and energy. On any given day, you may be asked to take on a task, favor, or social obligation that you're not comfortable with—either because you don't have the time or you just don't want to do it. Perhaps the request doesn't align with your goals, values, or beliefs, or it could be that you're currently inundated with other obligations. Whatever the reason, you know you want to say no, but you fear upsetting the other person.

This kind of approval-seeking behavior disregards your own needs and increases your stress level. You're never going to be able to please everyone, especially as you begin to level up and your decisions become more aligned with what you need versus what's best for everyone else.

Though it can be quite an uncomfortable feeling, learning to accept disapproval and the discomfort that comes with it is part of leveling up your mental toughness. It reduces stress related to time management and relationships.

TAKE IT TO THE NEXT LEVEL

Come back to this exercise the next time you're asked to do something and feel torn about how to respond. First, try to tap into that intuitive place that knows right away whether or not something is good for you. If you're still not sure, ask yourself the following:

- Do I have time for this?
- Will this task add to my life or add to my stress?

- Why is it so hard to say no to this?
- Is this something I want to do?
- Is this something I hate doing?
- Will it bring me closer to something I want?

Then try these tips for saying no:

1. If you're unsure if it's a yes or a no, take at least one day to think about it. You can say, "Let me think about it," or "Let me check my schedule and get back to you."
2. Practice saying no to simple things first, and then build your way up to harder situations.
3. Be assertive and clear, while still being respectful.
4. If you decide to offer an explanation, do so in a positive manner. Make it concise, and avoid overexplaining or overapologizing.
5. Thank the person who asked for the favor; let them know you're flattered.

Saying no takes practice, but the more you do it, the easier it gets. You'll find that the decreased stress in your life will be more than worth the initial discomfort.

EXERCISE 70:
CREATE A POSITIVE ANCHOR

There are many wonderful techniques for promoting relaxation and relieving stress, such as practicing yoga, meditating, or taking a hot bath. But sometimes in the heat of the moment, you need to alleviate stress quickly in order to stay calm and focused on the task at hand—for example, in a job interview or during a serious discussion with someone. One effective way to ease some stress instantly is to use the power of your senses.

Have you ever had the experience of hearing a song on the radio followed by a sudden reversal in your mood? Let's say that song was playing when you and your ex broke up. It was a very sad day. Years later, whenever you hear that song, memories come flooding back and you feel sad. You have that strong emotional response because your brain anchored your emotion to the sounds of that song. An anchor is a sensory stimulus that always causes a specific reaction in a person. Anchors work the same for all your senses, not just hearing. Maybe it's the smell of the fragrance your ex was wearing, or the sight of a sports hat like the one your ex wore on that fated day.

The good news is that anchors can also lift you up. They're not only formed during difficult times in your life; they're also created when you experience a peak emotional state. For example, whenever you smell maple syrup, you're reminded of Sunday mornings at your grandma's house. You consequently feel a sense of joy wash over you. You can create and use anchors to help you move from chaos to calm in an instant.

TAKE IT TO THE NEXT LEVEL

Follow these steps to create an anchor that helps you overcome stress and find your calm center:

1. Find a quiet place where you can be alone.
2. Close your eyes and think back to a positive past experience that had you in an incredibly calm, happy state of mind. Recall this memory as vividly as possible, imagining how you felt, what you saw, heard, smelled—maybe touched and/or tasted.
3. At the peak intensity of reliving this peaceful moment, make a hand gesture that you normally wouldn't make. Some examples: pressing two specific fingertips together, pulling on your earlobe, or rubbing your hands together.
4. Repeat this process every day, or even multiple times a day, for as long as it takes to anchor this emotional state to the specific hand gesture.
5. Once you've repeated the process many times, you can test to see if the anchor is working. When you're feeling stressed, try using the hand gesture to quickly take you back to that place of calm. If it doesn't do anything for you, continue steps 1 to 4 for a few more weeks and try again.

With practice, strong and positive anchors can help you get through and even thrive under pressure.

EXERCISE 71:
FIND TIME TO MOVE

Everyone knows how important it is to take care of their body, nurturing it with good food, exercise, and ample sleep. This helps ward off illness and keeps you generally healthy. But did you know that physical exercise is equally important for your mental health? When you enhance your physical fitness, you enhance your cognitive fitness! This includes—but is not limited to—your ability to reason, problem-solve, focus, adapt, and make sound decisions, all of which are vital components of a mindset that handles stress like a champ.

Without getting too scientific about it, exercise benefits the brain by improving blood flow, pumping in more oxygen, promoting plasticity (the brain's ability to change), and lowering levels of stress hormones! While aerobic exercise, resistance training, and mind-body exercises are all associated with improvements in cognitive functioning, exercise in almost any form can act as a stress reliever.

Most people already know how beneficial exercise is for their mental well-being, but they feel too busy and stressed to fit it into their routine. If you think there's no room in your day for exercise, take heed: Physical activity is more accessible than you think! With a little creativity and determination, it's easy to find pockets of time every single day to move your body.

TAKE IT TO THE NEXT LEVEL

For at least one week, work some of the following activities (or your own) into your routine.

Don't get fixated on how many minutes you're exercising. If you pick a handful of these activities to commit to for the week, you'll have moved your body that much more than you otherwise would have. After one week, see if you notice any results in your brain health.

- Take the stairs instead of the elevator
- Propose walking meetings with coworkers and/or clients
- Take short breaks from work for a quick power walk around the block or up a flight of stairs
- Do sit-ups while you watch TV
- Trade drinks with friends for a game of tennis, a hike, or a dance class
- Take a quick, brisk walk after dinner
- Turn chores into a workout by moving more vigorously while vacuuming, or running up a flight of stairs when you switch between tasks

A note for those with physical limitations: It's not easy for some people to engage in a "normal" level of physical activity. Those with existing health issues, pain, or injuries may think they don't have a lot of options, but there's almost always some way to stimulate your cardiovascular system. Do a little research and find out what options exist for you.

EXERCISE 72:
EXTERNALIZE YOUR ANXIETY

Everyone deals with uncomfortable feelings like anxiety on occasion. Mental toughness is displayed in how you approach these feelings—not by lacking them. The greatest performers on earth may feel anxiety before a competition, but they're able to reframe their inner dialogue and choose their response.

Anxiety is meant to keep you safe from threat, but a lot of the time you're not actually in any real danger. Your thesis isn't going to attack you, and bombing your presentation isn't going to kill you. If you always listen to what your anxiety is saying to you, you may miss out on some great opportunities.

Since anxiety is your specific reaction to stress, its origin is internal, making it hard to differentiate yourself from it. You may feel like it's part of your personality, but actually, it's just a feeling that will come and go! One way to deal with anxiety when it comes up is to externalize it. Imagine yourself in a battle against it and its symptoms.

TAKE IT TO THE NEXT LEVEL

You are not your anxiety. So externalize it—separate it from yourself! Try the following technique the next time you're struggling with anxious thoughts:

1. Name your anxiety and give it a voice. It's always trying to hold you back and drag you down, and honestly it's a bit of a jerk. So think of something or someone you don't like—say, your ex-boyfriend Steve—and name your

anxiety that! Let Steve be the narrator of your negative self-talk.

2. Identify how it makes you feel, think, and behave. For example, "Steve makes me feel like I can't attempt difficult things. He holds me back. He always makes me second-guess myself. I'm pretty sure he's going to show up at my race today and try to screw things up."

3. Confront it and tell it where to go! For example, "Okay, Steve, you can get lost now! We both know you're a liar and everything's going to be just fine."

Practice externalizing your anxiety this way until it becomes a more automatic process.

CHAPTER 8

EXERCISES TO FORGE SELF-CONFIDENCE

The most resilient, mentally tough people face setbacks with confidence. Even if they don't have the knowledge or prior experience needed to work through a particular problem, they maintain belief in their ability to figure it out. Of course, confidence is not something people are born with; it's built over the years, though it doesn't always happen in a linear fashion. When life knocks you down, your confidence can be deflated, and you may need to do a bit of work to build it back up. Other times, your confidence may continue to grow without setbacks. It's a process of peaks and valleys.

You may have more confidence in some areas of your life than in others, or have found your confidence to be generally lacking across most aspects…and that's okay! The exercises in this chapter are designed to help you develop your confidence in every realm and every type of situation you may face. It's time to cultivate a foundation of self-belief that will help you stay tough no matter what.

EXERCISE 73:
REWRITE YOUR STORY

What is the story you repeat to yourself over and over? You know, the one you've been telling yourself your entire life about who you are, what you're capable of, and how things always turn out for you. A lot of people have these stories, and most likely, the "story" you've created for yourself has a negative connotation to it. That's because the narrative is often full of self-limiting beliefs; for example, "Life is hard. Nobody understands me. Nothing ever works out for me." It shapes your sense of identity and internal narrative, and unfortunately keeps you stuck and thwarted from achieving your goals.

Mentally tough individuals have healthy core beliefs about themselves, other people, and the world around them. They know that mindset is key to achieving anything in life and that a healthy inner narrative is foundational to success. You need to have more beliefs that lift you up and motivate you than the ones that drag you down. A mentally tough person's storyline would be more like, "Life is good. People always like me. I can do anything I set my mind to."

Leveling up your own mental toughness means being aware of what you tell yourself. Would you say that negative stuff to your friends? Didn't think so. The good news is that there's always room to change your story.

TAKE IT TO THE NEXT LEVEL

Complete the following steps to identify your current narrative and create a new, motivational story in its place:

1. Identify your challenges. Think about the areas in your life where you feel most challenged or dissatisfied: relationships, health, career, etc. Chances are there are some limiting beliefs lingering around here. Within the areas you identified, make a list of the challenges that you're facing.
2. Identify the inner critic. For each challenge that you listed, think about the self-destructive thoughts and beliefs that may be contributing to this area, and write them down. For example, a destructive belief surrounding a relationship issue may be "I'm not good enough for that person."
3. Evaluate the storyline. Cross out any of the beliefs that seem insignificant or unimportant. You want to pinpoint which beliefs have the greatest negative impact on your life. What you're left with might be one sentence or it might be a few.
4. Write a new script. It's time to throw away your old story and write a new and healthier one. Your new story should look more like the opposite of the old story, and it will support your ability to improve your life. Notice when you may be acting from the old storyline and recite to yourself the new one.

EXERCISE 74:
WRITE A SELF-LOVE LIST

Being outwardly confident as you navigate the world around you starts from within. The value that you place on yourself helps facilitate the confidence you need to push through barriers. This value is known as self-love, and it's foundational to quieting your inner critic and making healthy choices. In fact, it has often been said that lack of self-love is at the root of all problems. So how do you cultivate your sense of worth in order to become more confident? By continually practicing the habit of nurturing and loving yourself unconditionally.

TAKE IT TO THE NEXT LEVEL

Make a list of all the things you love about yourself. There are no limits to what you can include. Any positive quality you possess that you appreciate or makes you feel proud should be written down on your list. These can include physical attributes, things you love about your personality, past accomplishments, ways you're working to improve, and issues you have overcome.

It may seem like a challenge to come up with all the things you love about yourself, and that's because it is. The hope is that you'll dig deep to uncover even those things you didn't know you loved about yourself.

You can return to this list anytime you're feeling low on confidence or just having a rough day. Never forget how far you've come and what you're capable of!

EXERCISE 75:
ASK, "AM I BEING TOO HARD ON MYSELF?"

Expectations are harmless, right? Wrong! Expectations can suck the life out of your confidence when you don't perform the way you think you "should" have. Sure, mental toughness requires that you demand a certain level of self-discipline, but it doesn't mean you should berate yourself if you haven't yet achieved your desired outcome. Remember that being tough means embracing challenges and even failures with an optimistic mindset! Reasonable expectations can be a useful tool for holding yourself accountable. But the more rigid the expectations you place on yourself, the more damaging they can be to your confidence if you don't meet them (not to mention the high levels of stress it can cause).

Confidence is void of strict expectations. To be successful you need to be confident in your abilities without the judgment that comes with shoulds.

TAKE IT TO THE NEXT LEVEL

Use the following steps to determine whether you are being too hard on yourself and adjust for more confidence:

1. Make a list of all the crazy expectations you have for yourself in different areas of your life. These can be expectations you have as a parent, friend, employee, and so on.
2. Go through your list and pretend these are expectations that you've placed on a loved one. One by one, decide

which of these expectations seem unreasonable or unfair to place on them. Cross those out!

3. Look at the new, more realistic list and let it be a lesson in the way you should treat yourself. You're not superhuman, so you shouldn't be expected to perform superhuman tasks. Let this list be a reminder that your best is good enough.

EXERCISE 76:
TURN YOUR INNER CRITIC
INTO YOUR INNER COACH

When faced with a difficult decision, you may hear two distinct, competing "voices" in your head. There's that optimistic, nurturing one who speaks with compassion and understanding, and then there's the mean and nasty one—the inner critic. While each has a role to play at different times, the critic that you have internalized over your lifetime can often go overboard when you've made a mistake. This monologue can completely undermine your confidence, reminding you of all the ways you're falling short. Also referred to as negative self-talk, the critic's voice is often very powerful and persistent.

By contrast, the other voice tends to be a little bit harder to hear. You can call this softer, more positive voice your inner coach. Because it isn't always obvious which voice you should listen to, the louder voice commonly wins. Building true mental toughness requires strengthening your nurturing inner coach and quieting that mean inner critic.

Because self-talk is a habitual way of thinking, it can be changed through practice, repetition, and persistence—by using more encouraging language with yourself and learning to tolerate the discomfort caused by quieting the negative self-talk that you're used to. As you lessen the power of your inner critic, you will begin to feel more confident with yourself and your decisions.

TAKE IT TO THE NEXT LEVEL

The following is a visualization exercise to help you find your inner coach. Check out the "Find Your Center" exercise in Chapter 7 to learn how to get centered before completing this exercise.

1. Picture your best future self—all the things you love and value about yourself now plus the things you hope to achieve in the future.
2. Once you have an image, take notice of all the physical attributes and personality traits of this best self. What does your best self look like? What are they wearing? Where and in what kind of home are they living? What is their routine like? What do they do for a living and for fun?
3. Once you've come up with a very clear picture of who this best self is, you have met your inner coach! This ideal future version of yourself is the person who should be guiding the decisions you make today. This mentor knows who you want to be and helps you grab hold of what you want.
4. Keep this visual of your inner coach and call on them the next time you're faced with your inner critic. Listen to what the coach has to say.

Your inner coach is the filter through which you should make your decisions from now on.

EXERCISE 77:
TAKE A SOCIAL MEDIA BREAK

Think back to the last time you compared yourself to someone else. How did it make you feel? Did it empower you and build up your confidence? Or did it make you feel discouraged or not quite good enough in some way?

As Theodore Roosevelt once said, "Comparison is the thief of joy." So why do people constantly rob themselves this way? When you compare your life and accomplishments to others, as you may while scrolling through social media, it can certainly bring up feelings of inadequacy. What's worse, you may forget that what you're seeing on your screen is only a small glimpse into someone's life—a filtered and curated glimpse, at that. Is what you're comparing yourself to even based in reality?

If you're feeling low on confidence, ask yourself why. Are you comparing yourself to others on a regular basis? Because there's only one person you should be comparing yourself to, and that's the person you were yesterday! If you feel good about your level of social media use, you may not need to do this exercise. But if any of this is resonating with you, it's time to level up and take back some control.

TAKE IT TO THE NEXT LEVEL

Follow these steps to end the comparison trap and refocus on things that build your confidence:

1. Create a social media post that tells your friends/followers you're taking a short break from social media. This will

help ease some of the anxiety you may be feeling about "going off the grid."

2. Delete your app(s) or temporarily deactivate your account(s). Depending on how far you want to take this and which outlets are doing more harm than good for you, you may want to cleanse yourself from one or all of your social media accounts.

3. Enjoy the newfound freedom from comparison for seven whole days. Take this time for extra self-care and reflection.

During your reflection, think about how and why you've been comparing yourself to strangers (or friends) on the Internet. Does it make sense to be comparing yourself to these people? Is there something in particular you're envious of? Are there specific goals you see others (apparently) achieving that you want for yourself? If so, start making a plan for achieving those goals. Also take some time during your cleanse to think about all the positive aspects of your life and personality.

While the main purpose of this exercise is to boost your confidence, you'll gain many other benefits. Social media cleanses are said to reduce anxiety, enhance focus, and help you reconnect with yourself. Come back to this exercise as many times as you see fit, taking a break from social media for a week at a time or even just one day every week.

EXERCISE 78:
FAKE IT TILL YOU MAKE IT

You've likely heard the aphorism "Fake it till you make it." It's when you act like the more confident person you wish you were in that moment. Although this strategy won't work in the long term, pretending to be more confident than you feel can help you to more easily slip into that role. As you practice the behavior that you want to adopt, eventually it will start to feel more natural!

One effective use of this strategy is to combat something known as "impostor syndrome." This confidence underminer is a belief that your successes are the product of luck or fraud rather than skill. It can be a crippling feeling. Imagine you feel under-qualified for a promotion you've gotten. Every time you speak to a client, you feel paralyzed at the thought of them finding out you don't know what the heck you're doing, when in fact, you are qualified and deserving of that promotion. Some of the greatest minds of all time were insecure about their talents and abilities at some point. It happens to everyone!

To be clear, this isn't an excuse to be a phony. Never lie about your core skills or abilities. This strategy should be used with good intentions—when you've identified something within yourself that's holding you back from being the most successful you.

TAKE IT TO THE NEXT LEVEL

Pick an area of your life where a lack of confidence might be affecting your performance—whether it be at work, on the sports field, dating, you name it. Now grab your notebook and reflect on the following questions: If you were to act like you had unlimited confidence in _____ (your area of interest), what would that look like? In other words, how would you behave differently with this newfound confidence? How would you walk, talk, and carry yourself? How would your performance be different? How would you talk to yourself? How would you treat others, and they you? What kinds of things would you start doing? What would you stop doing? How would your goals change?

After you've reflected on these questions for some time, go out there and fake it till you make it! Swallow your fear and act as though you're the most confident person there is. Remember your insights from previous questions, work on changing the behavior, and trust that the feelings will follow. With every opportunity, act like this successful, confident person, and your confidence in your abilities will increase.

EXERCISE 79: SEE YOURSELF AS OTHERS SEE YOU

All too often, people worry about what others think of them. They're concerned with what others think about their capabilities, personality, intelligence, physique, and more. But this worry is completely unproductive. An internal dialogue of the worst things someone could potentially think or say about you is a surefire way to kill your confidence. Besides the fact that much of it is likely to be untrue (you are your own worst critic, after all), these assumptions serve no purpose in your life.

Have you ever stopped to compare what you think other people think of you to your own self-limiting beliefs and biases?

You'd be surprised at how much of these worries are actually more about what *you* think of you. Your self-image doesn't always line up with others' image of you, especially if you're low on confidence. To embody mental toughness, you have to go after the things you want with self-belief. Without the confidence to back you, it's going to be a lot harder to take action and stick to your goals. Have a look at the image you've created for yourself. Does it need a little tweaking?

TAKE IT TO THE NEXT LEVEL

Pick a handful of people you come into contact with most. Try to make it a diverse mix: some family, some coworkers, some friends—all people who know you pretty well, of course. Ask them to tell you their favorite three qualities about you. You'll find that these people will have genuine things to say about you that may conflict with your own self-image. Becoming aware of these discrepancies is a great way to shake up the image you have of yourself and boost your confidence.

EXERCISE 80:
LEARN A NEW SKILL

Need a confidence boost? Learn something new! Learning how to do something you couldn't do before is rewarding on so many levels. Not only will it bring new skills, but it can also help you realize that you're capable of more than you ever expected!

Deciding you're going to attempt something for the very first time also takes guts. You know that at the beginning you may not be very good, and it might be a little uncomfortable. Practicing this sort of discomfort is a good thing, and it will give you the confidence to take chances in other areas of your life as well. And when you're able to talk fluidly about a new subject, you may feel more confident in your social skills to have conversations in general. You may even decide you want to further your education!

So whether you've always wanted to learn Spanish or how to play the drums, there's no better time than now.

TAKE IT TO THE NEXT LEVEL

Is there anything you've always been curious or passionate about, maybe even since childhood? Or perhaps there's a course you've been wanting to take online, or a creative project you keep daydreaming about.

If you're ready to commit even just a little bit of time to some ongoing learning, give it a shot! And while you can come up with a goal for developing this new skill, you can also just do it for the joy of learning. Try to work it into your routine so that you make steady progress, but don't get down on yourself if things get complicated or life gets busy. If you find yourself succumbing to any negative self-talk, bring your awareness back to why you're doing this in the first place: to boost your confidence. Have fun!

EXERCISE 81:
CREATE YOUR OWN ELEVATOR PITCH

Have you ever bumped into an old boss or client, or maybe an ex-lover or friend, and found yourself at a loss for words? Responding to "So tell me about yourself" or "What have you been up to lately?" can be a surprisingly daunting task when you're not prepared. Your confidence can take a hit when you feel you have nothing noteworthy to say about your life. But you do—you're just being put on the spot!

An elevator pitch is a succinct and snappy way of introducing yourself that captures the attention of the listener. It's a quick summary of who you are and what you have to offer, often highlighting your proudest moments, interesting facts, and/or unique and positive characteristics. Elevator pitches are generally used in the business world to pique someone's interest or make a new connection, but elevator pitches can also come in handy in less formal social situations. The traditional pitch answers the question, "If you were in an elevator with someone who could move your career forward, what would you say to them in the thirty to sixty seconds available before the elevator doors reopen and they disappear?" Here's an example of an effective elevator pitch:

> I've been a sales director for eight years now, and if there's one thing I've learned, it's to listen more than you speak. I listen when my clients tell me their pain points—and I mean really listen. Ask any of my clients and they'll tell you that if I can't find a solution to their problem, I'll find someone who can. I'm currently managing a $5 million territory and

recently closed the single largest regional deal in the company's history. I'm known among colleagues for my democratic leadership style and fun-loving personality, and though I really enjoy my current job and team, I'm ready to expand into an upper management role. If you could use a guy like me on your team, give me a call!

Have your own pitch prepared, and you will be ready to exude confidence when the moment comes.

TAKE IT TO THE NEXT LEVEL

Follow these steps to create your own elevator pitch:

1. Establish your purpose for the pitch. Is it for networking, interviewing, dating (think dating app profile), or something else? Remember that you can tailor different versions for different occasions.
2. In as few words as possible, highlight your recent achievements, what you're up to, what you're looking for, and what you have to offer. Make it interesting!
3. Be clear and confident in your delivery and make it brief (thirty to sixty seconds).
4. Include an invitation to continue the conversation (if you so desire).

EXERCISE 82: HONE YOUR INTUITION

People often struggle with the concept of making decisions based on "intuition." This word is in quotation marks here because it's such a misunderstood concept. What some people might think is New Age nonsense is actually a powerful skill backed by science. Though intuition is the ability to understand something without logical reasoning, it's based on past experiences, perspective, and accumulated knowledge. Unfortunately, people are often trained to ignore intuition and stick with logic. ·

Steve Jobs said, "Intuition is a powerful thing, more powerful than intellect, in my opinion," while entrepreneur Richard Branson relies "far more on gut instinct than researching huge amounts of statistics." Intuitive ability doesn't replace the need for logic; it complements it and helps people make better decisions with more confidence. It takes courage to trust yourself in such a big way, and that's the most important aspect of confidence—trusting yourself!

The weird feeling in your stomach, the little voice in your head—these are your gut instincts trying to tell you something. The more you practice listening, the stronger your intuition will become and the more confidence you will have in your inner voice. One of the most important things to do when trying to hear your guiding voice is to give yourself some distance from the problem. People tend to fixate on a problem until it's solved, but that's not how intuition works. Clear your head, stop ruminating over the matter, and the answer will come when you're ready to see it.

TAKE IT TO THE NEXT LEVEL

Here's a simple "snap decision" exercise to start developing your intuition:

1. Bring to mind a decision you've been deliberating.
2. Write the decision down on a piece of paper as an actionable question that requires a yes or no answer. For example, "Should I move out?" Underneath the question, write "yes/no."
3. Set the paper down with a pen next to it and go do something else for at least one hour. Try to put the question completely out of your mind!
4. Go back to the piece of paper, grab the pen, and close your eyes for a moment. Then open your eyes and, without hesitation, circle "yes" or "no."
5. Whatever you circled is your gut instinct.

If you couldn't get your mind off the question during your time away from the paper, or if you hesitated at all when selecting your answer, then scrap it and try again another day. And if you do have to repeat the exercise, try to change the words around a bit so your brain doesn't immediately register the same question and answer.

EXERCISE 83:
INITIATE A DIFFICULT CONVERSATION

No one likes conflict, but when a problem doesn't get addressed, it persists. It comes down to whether or not you're prepared to have difficult conversations. Many people avoid them at all costs, hoping the issue will go away on its own. One of the main reasons behind this avoidance is a lack of confidence in their ability to successfully navigate that conversation, which they mask behind the excuse "I just don't like confrontation."

No, confrontation isn't pleasant. Yes, the fear of an uncertain outcome is real. Initiating a delicate conversation can be super awkward and uncomfortable in the short term, but it will address an important issue. And the way to grow your confidence in having challenging conversations is to practice! Have a strategy, be prepared, and reframe the situation.

TAKE IT TO THE NEXT LEVEL

Think about someone with whom you might have a tough (but beneficial) conversation. It can be a friend, family member, or coworker. Then try to reframe the situation by pondering the following questions:

- Who is impacted by your not having the conversation?
- What's the best outcome you can expect if you never deal with the issue?
- What's the worst outcome you can expect if you never deal with the issue?

People tend to overestimate the cost of having difficult conversations and underestimate the effect of unresolved conflict on their well-being. Weigh the pros and cons. If you feel ready, initiate the conversation with them. If you don't feel quite ready, imagine how that conversation might go as a good first step.

EXERCISE 84:
UNPACK YOUR SHAME DRAWER

Shame corrodes the very part of us that believes we are capable of change.

—BRENÉ BROWN

Let this quote sink in for a minute. What Brown is talking about here is very important, since at the very root of mental toughness is the self-belief in one's ability to level up!

Shame is one of the most crippling emotions a person can have. It's activated every time you do something that has been labeled by others as wrong or disgraceful. Like many of the stories you tell yourself, a shame story can be based on something that was said to you in early life, and can stay with you for a very long time, drastically impacting your self-confidence and potential.

Most people have at least one thing they are ashamed of that they believe makes them fundamentally flawed and unworthy. The problem with shame is that when you ignore or avoid it, it often sneaks its way into many aspects of your life, creating distorted patterns of thinking. Conversely, sharing your shame experience with someone you trust can reduce your feelings of unworthiness and provide a much-needed reality check. Often, an outside perspective is just what you need to break free from whatever old story is causing you shame.

TAKE IT TO THE NEXT LEVEL

For this exercise, you're going to unpack your "drawer" of shame and show someone what's inside. Pick a trusted friend and let them in on your secret. Your friend may even feel motivated to share their shame story in return, helping you to see that you're not alone and that most people have some sort of shame hidden within.

CHAPTER 9

EXERCISES TO IMPROVE SELF-AWARENESS

Self-awareness, or the ability to see yourself clearly and objectively through reflection and introspection, is a crucial building block for emotional intelligence—and thus mental strength. You need some degree of self-awareness in order to react to what life throws at you in effective, healthy ways. There are two key types of self-awareness: internal and external. Internal self-awareness is about how clearly you're able to see your values, emotional triggers, strengths, and weaknesses; it impacts your decisions and overall success. External self-awareness is your understanding of how others perceive you; it plays a big role in mutually beneficial relationships. It's easy to assume that having a lot of one type of awareness means having a lot of the other, but that's not the case. Highly self-aware people actively focus on balancing both sides. It takes effort and practice.

You absolutely cannot level up without self-awareness. So it's time to build yours! In this chapter, you will explore the different core parts of who you are and what you desire in life. You'll take a deeper look at your strengths, as well as what you could improve, both through self-reflection and gaining an outsider's perspective. You will also take key steps toward being your best self, including asking for constructive criticism.

EXERCISE 85:
KNOW YOUR VALUES

Highly self-aware people are attuned to their core values and make a habit of regularly reflecting on them. Core values are the innermost truth of what is important to you. They're the principles that give meaning to your life, and help you persevere through hardship. They encompass many domains, including friendship, romance, service, and career success.

Mentally tough people use their values as guidelines to help them determine their priorities and make critical decisions confidently. Living in alignment with your values can not only give you a sense of inner peace and fulfillment—it can also reduce stress and help you respond to life in constructive ways.

It's time to get super clear about what's really important to you! Establishing a set of core values will enhance your self-awareness and help you live more intentionally.

TAKE IT TO THE NEXT LEVEL

Use the following steps to determine your personal values:

1. Recall a moment where you felt totally yourself: joyful, in your element, connected, fulfilled, aligned. Take some detailed notes in your notebook that describe this pinnacle moment.
2. Now think about why you enjoyed this moment so much. What values were being expressed and felt in that moment? Write them down. You can also visit

https://jamesclear.com/core-values for an extensive list of values to help you complete this step.

3. From the list you come up with, select one or two values that are the most important to you.

4. Repeat steps 1 to 3 until you have a set of five to seven different values that truly define who you are and what is most important to you. These are called your core values.

Once you have discovered your core values, you can start putting them into practice through deliberate reflection and goal setting (see the "Align Your Goals and Values" exercise in Chapter 2). Commit them to memory and start living in accordance with them!

EXERCISE 86: ASK "WHAT?" NOT "WHY?"

All too often, when people are trying to assess their current situation, they ask the question why: "Why is this happening to me?" "Why am I so upset?" "Why didn't I get the promotion?" "Why don't they like me?"

The problem with self-evaluation through asking why is that it can be very unproductive. First, this type of introspection has a tendency to highlight the negatives, which can cause you to focus on your limitations. Second, you don't have access to a lot of your unconscious thoughts and motives, so you're likely to get it wrong.

Instead, highly self-aware people ask a much more productive question, which encourages more positive introspection: what. What questions encourage you to use practical information and consider the causes for current situations? This will allow you to remain more objective, internalize less, and recognize the factors that are out of your control so you can re-strategize.

TAKE IT TO THE NEXT LEVEL

For this exercise, consider something you're currently going through—something that's had you asking a lot of *why* questions—and write a quick journal entry about it. Then, use the following *what* questions (and any other ones you can think of) to help you objectively look at the situation from a different perspective:

- What emotions am I feeling?
- What caused me to feel this way?
- What thoughts am I having?
- What made me think this?
- What reactions am I experiencing?

Use these questions and your journal reflection to gain more insight into what is really happening. You may be surprised at what comes up!

EXERCISE 87:
IDENTIFY YOUR WORST HABITS

The first step toward building better mental habits—and a big part of understanding yourself—is becoming aware of your bad habits. Mentally strong people know that once they eliminate their worst mental habits, the good ones become more effective.

Generally, you form mental habits without being consciously aware of them. The average person runs on autopilot all day long, using mental shortcuts that are helpful for quicker decision-making and problem-solving. But sometimes, this lack of awareness is not very useful. These mental shortcuts are often constructed from untrue or unhelpful beliefs and patterns based on past experiences, which negatively affects your emotions and behavior.

It's time to bring intentional awareness to your least helpful mental habits so that you can gain control of your mind and stop sabotaging yourself!

TAKE IT TO THE NEXT LEVEL
Follow these steps to uncover which habits are not serving you:

1. First, prime yourself by identifying some healthy habits. Ask yourself, "What is currently working in my life? What habits help me achieve happiness, success, and important goals?"
2. Then ask yourself, "What is not working in my life? What habits are currently holding me back from achieving happiness, success, and important goals?" These habits can

include making excuses, feeling guilty, thinking you're a failure, catastrophizing the future, seeking approval from others, and comparing yourself negatively with others. Identify your worst habits and write them down.

Throughout this book you'll find many opportunities to work on existing habits you'd like to change. Use the ones you've identified here. Also consider where you can insert more of the habits you identified in step 1 into your life.

EXERCISE 88: BORROW AN OUTSIDER'S PERSPECTIVE

One way to improve your self-awareness is to adopt an outside view of your life. How would an observer evaluate the life circumstances you're in or the challenges you're facing? What would they think about your struggles? About your successes? You're often too attached to your problems to be able to see them for what they really are. Embracing a fresh perspective removes your personal biases and emotions, enabling more objectivity. Generally people show more compassion to others than they do toward themselves, so an outsider's perspective can also be more optimistic, reducing stress and negative emotions.

TAKE IT TO THE NEXT LEVEL

Close your eyes and pretend that you're someone else looking in on your life. Maybe it's your neighbor you see often but don't speak to much. Or maybe you're a distant coworker. Grab your notebook and narrate the story of your life in the third person, from their perspective. When you are done, reflect on the things you wrote about yourself. What did you learn?

EXERCISE 89: ASK FOR CONSTRUCTIVE CRITICISM

Self-awareness doesn't stop at how you see yourself. Understanding how you're perceived by the people around you (external awareness) is an essential part of leveling up because it can show you where there is room for improvement. It's also important for building successful relationships, such as in the workplace. In this case, knowing how your employees see you can help you gain their trust and make you a more effective leader overall.

There's no better way to get a sense of how people perceive you than to simply ask them. Asking other people for feedback can help you uncover blind spots, as well as where you are doing a great job, so you can focus on improvement and keep up with good practices.

TAKE IT TO THE NEXT LEVEL

For this exercise you're going to ask someone for their honest feedback. Get specific; come up with a set of questions that will benefit you the most. Here are some examples:

- What do you think are my greatest strengths?
- What are my greatest weaknesses?

- If you had to describe me to someone, what would you say?
- Is there anything you avoid saying to me because you're afraid of how I'll react?
- What behaviors do you think are limiting my potential?

Try to follow these guidelines as you ask your questions:

- Ask someone who knows you well enough to have an informed opinion, and who will be willing to give you the honest feedback you deserve
- Be prepared, as sometimes honest feedback can sting; have a plan to say thank you, avoid defensiveness, and absorb the truth
- If you feel up to it, ask a second person the same questions—and then maybe another person after that
- If you ask more than one person, look for patterns in their feedback

EXERCISE 90:
FIND YOUR RESISTANCE

Procrastination is a beast. A simple Internet search of the word yields over fifty-seven million results of advice for overcoming it. Clearly, it's an issue for many people. And while you may find endless strategies for beating procrastination, if you don't understand the *why* behind your own personal struggles, you will never truly tame the beast!

Procrastination happens when your brain resists your best intentions. Though lack of motivation and self-control play a big role, there may be something deeper going on. When you attempt to level up some part of yourself, you experience a psychological reaction to change that's known as resistance. This natural tendency to resist change is very common and has been experienced by everyone at one point or another. Just think of the adage "Old habits die hard."

Mental resistance is like a self-protection mechanism for the part of the brain that wants to continue to use its familiar programming. While this is an efficient way for the brain to perform routine habits, it compels you to act in ways that sabotage your goals and keep you stuck, which manifests as procrastination. The discomfort of change may stimulate reactions in the brain like fear, anger, denial, and confusion. (This all occurs at the subconscious level!)

Mental toughness means overcoming the circumstances that prevent you from succeeding. In order to bridge the gap between intention and action, you must become aware of the mental process of change, including what triggers your own resistance response, so you can make a plan to overcome those obstacles.

TAKE IT TO THE NEXT LEVEL

Over the next week, try to recognize the areas of your life where you might be resisting change, and which situations trigger you to procrastinate. Keep track of them in your notebook.

Resistance can look like:

- Getting distracted
- Giving in to temptation
- Wasting time
- Making excuses

- Overthinking
- Giving up
- Perfectionism

Some areas of resistance might be easier to spot than others, so make it your intention to actively look for it in your life. Take notes so you can track any patterns! It might help to write the word *resistance* on a sticky note and place it somewhere that you'll notice throughout the day—like your desk, computer, refrigerator, TV, or bathroom mirror—so you'll be reminded to watch for the ways you are resisting.

At the end of the week, explore any patterns you may have noticed. What have you learned about yourself during this process? How can you utilize these insights to level up?

EXERCISE 91: BEFRIEND YOUR SHADOW

Everyone has an image of themselves that was formed through the repeated experiences they had with others. Over the course of your childhood, society, your parents, your friends, your teachers, and others taught you how you were supposed to be and how you were not supposed to be. Traits that were associated with being "good" were accepted, while traits associated with being "bad" were rejected. You were encouraged and shown how to be "normal." Through this process, you formed your sense of identity in the world.

Those aspects of your personality that may have been rejected by others were repressed over the years and became unconscious to you. They're collectively known as your "shadow self"—the part of you that's incompatible with the sense of identity you have cultivated and referred to as the "dark side" of your personality. The shadow self consists primarily of negative emotions and attributes, like rage, greed, hate, laziness, and selfishness.

However, your shadow self is what you *perceive* as needing to be hidden, so depending on your early life experiences and level of self-esteem, it might very well be hiding some of your greatest potential! Things like independence, emotional sensitivity, creativity, introversion, and more may have been discouraged during your formative years and can actually be wonderful parts of your personality.

Interestingly, you tend to see the qualities you deny yourself in others. Like a mirror, you project your shadow qualities onto the people you encounter in your life, subconsciously expecting them to suppress these perceived bad traits just as you do. As renowned psychiatrist Carl Jung once said, "Everything that irritates us about others can lead us to an understanding of ourselves."

Mental toughness involves facing uncomfortable truths about yourself with honesty and courage. With effort, honesty, and courage, you can become aware of your shadow self and learn to embrace it.

TAKE IT TO THE NEXT LEVEL

Reflect on what you've just read about the shadow self. Do you intuitively have an idea of what's hiding in your shadow? If not, that's okay. This is courageous work that takes continued effort!

Then start paying attention to your emotional reactions toward other people. The next time somebody causes a strong emotional reaction in you, take notice. After that encounter, use your notebook to reflect on the following questions about the person who frustrated/annoyed/upset you:

- What quality or qualities about this person did you find so annoying/upsetting?
- Do you have any idea why you find these qualities so irritating?
- In what ways/areas of your life might you sometimes display those same attributes?

Practice getting in touch with these qualities that you're fighting so hard to push out of your experience, and work on accepting them. Recognize that everyone possesses the same range of human emotions, whether they engage with them all the time or not. And that includes you! Practice acceptance.

EXERCISE 92: DISCOVER YOUR STRENGTHS

In the endless pursuit of self-improvement, it's easy to get caught up in your weaknesses because they're the things you need to work on. Meanwhile, you assume your strengths don't need any attention. But this is far from the truth. Your strengths are the value you bring to the world—not owning them is actually doing a disservice to those around you. As expert in positive psychology Alex Linley said, "Realizing our strengths is the smallest thing we can do to make the most difference."

If someone were to ask what your greatest strengths were, would you be able to answer? Or would the question challenge you or make you feel uneasy? Many people don't feel comfortable tooting their own horn, and it's surprising how many others don't even know what skills they possess.

Being mentally tough means knowing every part of yourself, especially what you are good at. These strengths are your most powerful tools for success. When you know what they are and how to leverage them, you can reach your goals with greater ease.

TAKE IT TO THE NEXT LEVEL

If you can confidently name your greatest strengths—fantastic! Otherwise, there are strengths-based assessments you can use to discover your unique collection of personal abilities. One of the most popular assessments is the VIA Character Strength Survey developed by Martin Seligman and Christopher Peterson. It can be found online at www.viacharacter.org and takes about fifteen minutes to complete.

Use this survey to identify your core strengths, then pick the strength that you least knew you had and find a way to use it every day for one week. Having greater awareness of your skills is a great way to boost your confidence and increase your chances of success.

EXERCISE 93:
WRITE YOUR OWN EULOGY

Don't let the title of this exercise scare you. Its aim is to give you a sense of perspective about what really matters to you. Many people go through their lives unsure of what they hope to accomplish in their time on earth. They never take the time to gain clarity. But thinking about this can help you reconnect with yourself and provide a sense of urgency for you to take action toward your dreams.

Reflect on your life experiences and how they've shaped you. Are you satisfied with where you are? Do you have a sense of purpose? If you died tomorrow, would you be proud of the legacy you'd leave behind? How do you want to be remembered? Are you living in accordance with that, right now? Use this opportunity to make sure you're on a path to fulfillment, not one of regrets about things left undone.

TAKE IT TO THE NEXT LEVEL

Use these questions to guide you as you write your own eulogy:

- What words best describe your life?
- What are your proudest accomplishments?
- What character traits do you want to be celebrated by those you leave behind?
- Who was the real you all along?
- What has life meant to you?
- What is your favorite memory?
- How did you make the world a better place?

- What did you say no to?
- How would you like your loved ones to honor your memory?

EXERCISE 94: INTERVIEW YOURSELF

Self-awareness is one of the keys to personal growth, productivity, success, and happiness—but it's also one of the most difficult things you can master. While you may be deeply connected to how you feel, feelings are highly subjective and can sometimes lead you to false beliefs.

If you want to understand yourself more deeply, it can be useful to have a conversation with yourself. Think about how you would get to know someone else: You'd spend time with them, observe, and ask them open-ended questions. This is your chance to have a face-to-face interview to understand the real you.

TAKE IT TO THE NEXT LEVEL

Feel free to answer all of these questions, pick the ones that feel most relevant to you, or even customize them. As always, the more effort you put in, the more rewarding you'll find this exercise to be. Try to make this time "sacred"—dedicated exclusively to focusing on you. Find a nice, quiet place that perhaps inspires you, and make yourself unreachable (no distractions!). Different people will interpret these questions in different ways. Don't overanalyze; just go with the first response that pops up in your mind. There are no right or wrong answers here.

- What three words best describe you?
- What do you love about yourself?
- What is your biggest strength?
- What is your biggest weakness?
- What makes you tired?
- What energizes you?
- What stresses you out?
- What relaxes you?
- What makes you happy?
- What makes you sad?
- What makes you angry?
- What are you most afraid of?
- Are your decisions generally based more on logic or emotion?
- What type of friend do you want to be? Partner? Family member?
- How do you want others to see you?
- What is your definition of success?
- What is your biggest dream?
- What makes this dream worth fighting for?
- What is standing in your way?
- Who are the most important people in your life?
- What are your priorities at the moment?
- What do you need more of in your life?
- What is bothering or worrying you at the moment?
- What are you grateful for?

Some of these answers may inform you how best to use the other exercises in this book, or what areas you most need to work on overall in your life.

EXERCISE 95: KEEP A JOURNAL

When you were growing up, you may have kept a diary or journal stashed away in a secret hiding spot where no one could ever find it. You turned to your journal to write down your secrets, dreams, misfortunes, and creative ideas. There were no rules to what you could put in your journal as a kid, and the same applies today! Some of the greatest minds throughout history kept journals—Maya Angelou, Thomas Edison, Albert Einstein, and Frida Kahlo, to name a few.

There's no substitution for self-reflection. Knowing your strengths and weaknesses, your dreams and ambitions, habits, patterns, and everything in between is essential for leveling up on mental toughness. But sometimes this information stays hidden from you, just beneath the surface of conscious awareness. The act of journaling can bring these things to the surface to be explored. What's causing this anxiety? Why am I behaving this way? Having a judgment-free place to sort your thoughts can help you make difficult decisions and bring clarity when you need it most.

Another benefit to keeping a journal is the ability to go backward and see what your frame of mind was during a certain period in your life. You can see how you worked through a decision process or how you dealt with a particular relationship issue. Working backward provides deep and meaningful insights that you can use in the present! Even more, the simple act of writing down your thoughts and feelings can be a welcome, cathartic release—a healthy outlet for processing uncomfortable emotions (see the "Try Expressive Writing" exercise in Chapter 3 for more on this).

A journal differs from your mental toughness notebook, as your notebook is a place to address specific questions and exercises. Your journal, however, is a place to openly express whatever you're thinking and feeling—free from rules, structure, or any particular agenda.

TAKE IT TO THE NEXT LEVEL

Using a dedicated notebook for free-style journaling, give it a go for one week. After seven days, if you decide that journaling isn't for you, no problem! If you do see the value in making it a regular practice, you may want to combine it with the "Cultivate Gratitude and Set Your Intentions" practice from Chapter 6, to keep all your heartfelt writing in one place.

There are no set rules for journaling, but here are a few guidelines that you may find useful:

1. Try to stick to pen and paper. Science says the brain digests information better when it's handwritten rather than typed.
2. Write every day. Schedule a time for it—such as first thing in the morning or just before bed—so you're more likely to stick with the process.

3. Don't worry about spelling, grammar, or sentence structure. No one will ever read this journal but you!

4. Write whatever feels right. You can recap your day, talk about your feelings, explore your problems, or all of the above.

5. Consider journal prompts if you don't know what to write about. There are plenty of these online; simply search for "journaling prompts."

EXERCISE 96:
ASK, "WHO AM I?"

Who am I? It's one of life's most defining questions. And it's easy to go through your days without ever deliberately answering this question. However, it's an important one to consider. From the choices you make to the values you live by, your sense of identity steers your life path and helps equip you mentally for whatever comes your way.

So, who are you?

The truth is, this question isn't meant to produce a definite answer. Instead, it's meant to lead you down a path of self-discovery, uncovering truths that can bring more clarity and direction to your life. Through contemplation, you may realize where you want to put more of your energy, or perhaps where you should be spending less. Discovering who you are is a never-ending journey. You're always changing and evolving, so learning about your identity is an ongoing process. Use this question to notice how you identify yourself and to get to know yourself apart from how everyone else sees you.

TAKE IT TO THE NEXT LEVEL

Find a quiet place for some undisturbed introspection. Ask yourself, "Who am I?" Simply see what answers come back to you. Use your notebook to reflect.

CHAPTER 10

EXERCISES TO EMBRACE FAILURE

Sometimes the fear of failure can overshadow your motivation to succeed, causing you to unconsciously undermine your efforts to achieve your dreams. Stepping outside of your comfort zone can feel very unnatural and often dredge up feelings of anxiety and physical discomfort. For these reasons, you may talk yourself out of trying entirely. However, mentally tough people understand that failing is part of the process; they see setbacks not as the opposite of success, but as the key to success! Inner strength involves taking calculated risks, assessing potential downsides before taking action, and knowing that failure is a learning experience.

Are you afraid to fail? That's okay! The exercises in this chapter help you embrace that fear and discomfort so you can take the risks that offer invaluable opportunities for growth. You'll practice a tougher response to setbacks and examine past mistakes for the value they have in your journey to success and happiness. So are you ready to level up and leave your fears behind? Let's get started.

EXERCISE 97:
LEARN FROM THE PAST

The less afraid you are of failing, the less likely you will be to fail. As Michelle Obama put it, "Failure is a feeling long before it becomes an actual result." The fear of failing is often irrational and based on past experiences as opposed to a logical assessment of the current situation and potential outcomes. If you take the time to analyze past failures and explore what you gained from them—rather than focusing solely on what you lost—you can begin to see the opportunity in them!

It's time to start seeing failure as a learning experience. This is not an easy skill to develop, but as you practice it, you'll get better and may even begin to find the process motivating.

TAKE IT TO THE NEXT LEVEL

To begin, dig back into your past and identify a time that you failed. You can jump straight to one of your biggest perceived failures, or you can start small with something that was less impactful. With your chosen experience in mind, answer the following three questions:

1. What did you learn from this experience?
2. How did you grow as a person from this experience?
3. What opportunities came about from this experience?

Your first attempt at answering these questions may be difficult, especially if the failure caused you a great deal of distress. If this is the case, close your eyes, practice some deep breathing to refocus yourself, and reattempt the questions. Before you know it, you'll have a list of positives that came from that perceived failure. Try this exercise a few more times using other examples from the past.

EXERCISE 98: PRACTICE FAILING ON PURPOSE

Everyone wants to succeed, but few are willing to fail in order to get there. The thing is, if you're not failing and making mistakes, you're not giving it your all. Mistakes teach you things you didn't previously know and bring you one step closer to succeeding.

Failing on purpose involves a comfort in taking calculated risks—a trait exhibited by the toughest individuals. They are not only willing to take the plunge into the unknown, but they're also comfortable with that jump. And getting comfortable with anything requires practice. Instead of feeling ashamed and scared of making mistakes, it's time to aim for them.

TAKE IT TO THE NEXT LEVEL

Set a goal to fail five times every month. Yes, you read that right. But before you freak out, keep in mind that failing simply means to fall short of a goal. You aren't ruining any chance of ever reaching that goal—just learning a bit more in order to reach its true potential in the future.

So set some goals that you'd be comfortable enough to fall short of. Keep track of your failures in your notebook, examining each one to see what you learned. Continue this practice for as long as it serves you. After some time you may notice that your willingness to fail has improved, and the distance between you and a certain goal has decreased.

EXERCISE 99:
ASK FOR HELP WHEN YOU NEED IT

Many people are willing to lend a helping hand, though few enjoy asking for it. There can be stigma attached to asking for help, especially in the workplace or other areas where you're expected to be highly skilled and confident. But guess what? Highly skilled, confident people see asking for help as a hallmark of maturity, humility, and mental strength. At the same time, the "helper" can see this as a courageous act and enjoy feelings of being valued and needed.

Life presents many challenges. Sometimes you need the support of your family, friends, managers, or coworkers to accomplish your goals. Rather than seeing this as a sign of weakness or incompetence, mentally tough people constantly seek to improve by any means possible. If that means sharing a problem with a trusted source who can help them achieve success, they will do so! Sometimes the only mistake you can make is not asking for help.

TAKE IT TO THE NEXT LEVEL

It's time to ask for help! Reflect on the following questions in your notebook:

1. Think of a time when you failed, in large part because you refused to ask for help.
2. Now think about a time that someone asked you for help. How did you feel about them asking? Did you provide the help? If so, were you happy to provide assistance, or did you feel negatively about it?
3. Consider where you can ask for help today. What situation might be improved by an extra hand (or perspective)?
4. Go on and ask for the help you need! Be selective and ask someone with the appropriate abilities, knowledge, and resources. Make it easy for them to help.

EXERCISE 100:
START BEFORE YOU FEEL READY

Perhaps one of the most underrated habits of the mentally tough is that they start before they feel completely ready. Like you, the most successful people in the world were once beginners. If they waited until conditions were perfect, they might never have gotten started. Whether you want to become an entrepreneur or you're looking to make a change in your personal life, at some point you have to take the first step. If you've been extensively planning something for a long time but don't feel ready to start anytime soon, chances are you're never going to feel ready.

There are several reasons why you may procrastinate getting started. The fear of failure—or of not getting it "just right" the first time—can be paralyzing. Embrace the idea of failure and know that some of your greatest learning will come from mistakes!

The more times you try, the more chances you have at success. Toss out the notion that there's going to be a perfect time to start something—there never is.

Don't feel confident in your abilities yet? Just by getting started, you'll begin to improve your confidence and self-belief. Let it be messy and imperfect. Let it be exciting and confusing at the same time. No matter what happens during this initial step, you'll be closer to reaching your goal because you have more insight and experience than you did before. If you want to level up and be a tougher person, sometimes you have to jump into action before you feel ready!

TAKE IT TO THE NEXT LEVEL

Pick one important thing that you haven't been able to start. You can go as small or as big as you want. Then:

1. Decide that it's worth the risk to start before you feel ready. Accept the discomfort or embarrassment you may be feeling. Know that you might get things wrong, and that's perfectly okay.

2. Make declarations, set up appointments, have conversations—anything that will hold you accountable to getting started.

3. Begin! You don't even need to have all the details figured out; just take the leap.

4. Enlist some "cheerleaders" who can support and encourage you along the way. You can ask friends to follow your new business account on social media and "like" and com-

ment on your posts. Or ask them to be an accountability buddy.

5. If at first you don't succeed, dust yourself off and try it again. No matter what happens, remember that you're not doing it "wrong"; you're just learning.

EXERCISE 101: BREAK THE MISTAKE CYCLE

Everyone makes mistakes! It's a part of being human. But when mistakes become recurrent, they're actually more like patterns. Is there a choice that you keep making over and over again, even though you consciously want to make a different, better choice? While your instinct might be to try to change the symptom (the behavior), you're likely going to keep coming up with the same results until you acknowledge the root cause of your pattern: Your unconscious biases/belief system.

Once a belief is formed, your brain will seek out evidence that supports that belief. In other words, you will subconsciously make decisions that align with that belief. For example, if deep down you believe that you have poor time-management skills, you might keep showing up late for work and important meetings. Or maybe you believe you're not worthy of unconditional love, so you continue to choose romantic partners who are emotionally unavailable. It's self-sabotaging behavior.

To break the cycle, you will need to take a step back and look at the bigger picture in order to get to the root of the problem.

When you understand your *why*, it makes the *how* a lot easier to implement.

TAKE IT TO THE NEXT LEVEL

Follow these steps to discover your mistake patterns and break the cycle of limiting beliefs and behaviors:

1. Identify a recurrent mistake that you want to stop making.
2. Stop beating yourself up for making this mistake. Instead of blaming yourself, acknowledge that it's a symptom of something bigger. Show yourself compassion and forgiveness.
3. Trace the mistake back to a negative belief, old emotional wound, or defense mechanism that tends to adversely affect your decisions. If you've already done the "Use Positive Affirmations" exercise (Chapter 6) or "Rewrite Your Story" exercise (Chapter 8), those insights could be extremely helpful here.

Hopefully, you're able to make some connections, but if not, that's okay! Now that you understand the concept, you can start to explore what might be going on internally. The best insights can come in the days and weeks after you've completed this exercise.

EXERCISE 102:
CALCULATE THE RISK

Every day, people stand in their own way of success by not taking risks. The truth is, risk is nothing to fear. It can be the difference between excelling in your goals and staying stagnant. This is not to say that you should take on any risk, however. Mental toughness involves the ability to properly assess a risk and to have the courage to take a chance on something when it makes sense to do so. Mentally tough people aren't just risk takers; they're calculated risk takers.

People often struggle with calculating risk, assuming that if it's really scary, it must be really risky. But the level of fear you experience has nothing to do with the actual level of risk. Fear will cause you to overestimate the danger. Conversely, the absence of fear will cause you to underestimate the risk. The assumption that something that isn't scary, isn't risky is also incorrect.

So how do you accurately determine which risks to take on and which ones are just not worth it? By examining the facts and balancing your emotions with logic. It's tricky to find this balance, as most people are naturally motivated by one side or the other, but with practice, you too can become a calculated risk taker and achieve more success in everything you put your mind to.

TAKE IT TO THE NEXT LEVEL

In your notebook, create a Venn diagram. Label the circle on the left "Logic," the circle on the right, "Feelings," and the overlapping section in the center, "Perceptions." Use the following steps to fill out the diagram to assess a risk in your professional or personal life:

1. Under "Logic," write down your rational assessment of the risk. This includes your research, maybe some pros and cons, common sense, or what experts you've spoken to said about it.
2. Under "Feelings," describe your intuitive feelings about the risk. What is your gut telling you?
3. Under "Perceptions," combine your logical and emotional assessments to create a balanced view of the situation. Try to understand where the emotions are coming from and how they affect your thinking and behavior.

A visual representation like this is just what you need to develop an understanding of where the two opposite forces of logic and emotion meet and the role they each play in a risk. Re-create this chart for each risk you need to assess.

EXERCISE 103: DETACH FROM THE OUTCOME

There's a way to approach goals with a more flexible attitude. Yes, you've chosen something meaningful to put your effort into, and you hope that by the end date, you will have accomplished something great…but what if you don't reach your goal? Essentially there are two ways of looking at it:

1. It's the end of the world. I failed. I blame myself/I blame x, y, or z. If I can't have this exact outcome, then I give up.
2. It's a bummer, but not the end of the world. I will learn from it and adjust my expectations to form a new goal. I am satisfied with my efforts.

Option 1 is the perception of someone who is rigidly attached to a specific outcome. There is a strong urge to control the circumstances and no room for error. Option 2 is the perception of someone who is outcome independent. Their definition of success is not tied to a specific outcome; it is flexible. They will roll with the punches.

Goals give you something tangible that you can strive toward, but certain factors are always going to be out of your control. To be more mentally tough, you must accept that and focus on solutions! By accepting that roadblocks and failures are a part of life, you won't be tempted to pass blame or play the victim. Detachment allows you to walk away with your head held high: You tried your best. You win some, you lose some. There's an incredible sense of freedom in this flexibility.

TAKE IT TO THE NEXT LEVEL

In the previous example, which one sounds more like you—option 1 or option 2? Think back and try to identify a time that you adopted each of these mindsets. How did things work out for you? Were you more resilient when you were attached to a specific outcome, or when you were outcome independent? Given these insights, are you ready to approach your goals with a more flexible attitude? What are you striving toward right now that could use an attitude adjustment?

EXERCISE 104: LEARN FROM OTHER PEOPLE'S FAILURES

Do you have any idea how many of the greatest success stories were fraught with failure? James Dyson designed 5,126 vacuum cleaners that didn't work before building the version that did. J.K. Rowling's *Harry Potter and the Philosopher's Stone* manuscript was rejected by twelve publishers before it finally was accepted. Each of their successes was only one outcome of many attempts.

You'll find hundreds more of these stories online, spanning every career path, hobby, and self-improvement journey you can think of. So while learning from your own mistakes is a useful exercise, why not also learn about the mistakes that others have made in a similar pursuit? It could not only save you time and money but also spare you the emotional toll of making that same mistake.

There's no need to reinvent the wheel. Before you begin any project, consider whether it's been done before, and apply any lessons learned. Try not to be so captivated by success, and put some of your energy into understanding what *hasn't* worked and why.

TAKE IT TO THE NEXT LEVEL

Can you think of someone who is currently succeeding at what you want to do? Do some research to find out how they got to where they are now. If it's someone you know or might be able to get in contact with, reach out to them and try to set up a meeting or quick phone call. You'd be surprised how willing people are to act as a mentor. Let them know that while you're fascinated by their success, you're more interested in hearing about any failures they experienced along the way.

If the person is no longer living or is difficult to get in contact with, see what you can dig up online. Or pick someone who is available to teach you a thing or two about how failure leads to success. How can you leverage their mistakes into your own success?

EXERCISE 105:
REFLECT ON THE RISKS YOU TOOK— AND THE ONES YOU DIDN'T

Life is a series of calculated risks—some you take, others you don't. No outcome is ever guaranteed, and failure is always possible. But sometimes the bigger risk is not taking one!

For some reason, certain risks just seem a lot scarier than others. Moving to another country, going back to school, switching careers at an older age, starting a business, getting married—all of these are examples of taking a chance that may result in huge payoffs. When you're afraid to fail, however, that fear can cloud your judgment. Maybe there was a time when you weren't so sure of yourself, and that impacted your decision. How do you feel about it in hindsight? Do you wish you had taken the chance? Do you wonder what might have been? To level up, you'll need to stop wondering. Stop allowing fear to dictate your choices, and take the leap to something that could bring greater success and happiness.

TAKE IT TO THE NEXT LEVEL

Grab your notebook and reflect on the biggest risks you've taken and the ones you haven't. Use these questions to guide your writing:

- What's the biggest risk you've ever taken?
- Why did you decide to take that risk?
- What might your life look like if you hadn't taken that risk?
- What's the biggest risk you chose not to take?
- Why did you decide not to take that risk?
- What might your life look like had you taken that risk?

Remember these insights the next time you're given the chance to take a risk.

EXERCISE 106: STOP AVOIDING FAILURE

Where your focus goes, your energy flows! Studies actually show that if you're focused on avoiding failure, you're more likely to fail.

The fixation on avoiding failure will cause you more stress and emotional turmoil than if you were focused on success. This can dampen your ability to think clearly and make good decisions. It can also give you tunnel vision, making you pay more attention to information that's pointing to failure and overlook other information that could move you in the direction of success. On the other hand, when you focus on the most successful outcome, you'll be thinking positive thoughts and are more likely to come up with creative solutions to your roadblocks.

At the end of the day, you can always decide what to focus on. A mentally tough person will seek and find opportunities and solutions. Someone with less resolve will focus on all that could go wrong. Take your pick!

TAKE IT TO THE NEXT LEVEL
Use your notebook to reflect on the following:

1. Where are you avoiding failure in your life right now?
2. Now flip it around: What potential successful outcome might you also be avoiding by not pursuing your desire? Write in detail about the most successful outcome you can imagine.
3. Ask yourself where you want to put your energy—into all the ways that you might fail, or all the ways that you might succeed?

EXERCISE 107:
FAIL BETTER

How you handle failure is far more important than how you handle success. When you know how to pick yourself up after getting knocked down, it makes the prospect of failing a lot less scary and drastically increases your chance of future success. A lot of it has to do with reframing the situation. Mentally tough people recognize that after the immediate sting of a setback, there's much to learn from it—and much to be proud of. If you've tried something and failed, you've succeeded at trying!

So what is your process for dealing with failure? If you aren't sure, now is the time to explore past experiences and start creating a plan to fail better in the future.

TAKE IT TO THE NEXT LEVEL

Take some time to reflect on your current response to failure. Ask yourself what you usually do when you make mistakes or fail at something and whether this is a constructive or negative approach. To better gauge whether your strategy is helpful, look at the following examples of negative responses to failure:

- Blaming yourself and questioning your capabilities
- Engaging in negative self-talk
- Trying to suppress uncomfortable emotions
- Taking it out on other people
- Dwelling on it
- Losing momentum
- Giving up

Are you guilty of any of these? If you determine that your usual response to failure isn't constructive to future success, you're ready for a change. The following steps will help you recover more quickly and effectively from a failure:

1. Accept an appropriate level of responsibility; own it.
2. Sort what's real from what's perceived (did you even fail?); acknowledge irrational beliefs.

3. Reframe the situation; look for the positives.
4. Allow your strong emotions to fuel your resolve.
5. Acknowledge what you did right.
6. Identify your weaknesses and how you can improve next time.
7. Use established coping strategies and take the time you need to recover.
8. Brainstorm new approaches.
9. Apply your learning and create a plan to try again!

Practice using these steps whenever you experience a setback.

EXERCISE 108: GET REJECTED

For some, the fear of failing is driven by a deeper fear of being rejected by others. This emotion can be crippling, affecting their ability to succeed in a wide range of personal and professional situations. After all, job interviews, business dealings, dating, and other situations are rife with the possibility of rejection. What if they don't like me? What if I make a fool of myself? What if they say no?

Rejection isn't a pleasant experience. In fact, it appears to activate the same brain regions that physical pain does! Naturally, avoidance is a common way to cope with this kind of fear, but it can result in many missed opportunities. When fear of rejection is too strong, it can hold you back from taking important risks and reaching for your dreams.

Mental toughness requires you to embrace the possibility of rejection. There will always be things that are out of your control—and the way other people respond to you is one of them. Not to worry, though, because you can use practical tools to shift your mindset and overcome your fear of rejection. One way is to purposely expose yourself to it. Practicing exposure to the very thing you're afraid of is an effective technique used in behavioral therapy.

TAKE IT TO THE NEXT LEVEL

Your challenge is to get rejected by someone at least once a day, every day, for one week. The idea is not to completely get rid of the shame or fear you have surrounding rejection, but to help you learn to live with those feelings.

Here are some ideas:

- Ask someone for a cigarette, some change, a piece of gum, or other item
- Ask a salesperson for a discount
- Ask someone for their phone number
- Pitch a wacky idea to your friends
- Ask someone out on a date

Put yourself out there. You will quickly learn that rejection is not going to ruin your life—but the fear of it might shut you out of a world of possibility.

CHAPTER 11

EXERCISES TO HONE ATTENTIONAL FOCUS

The ability to hone your focus and stay on task has become one of the most valuable skills in an increasingly fragmented world. Our attention spans are shrinking as many of us spend our days in an unintentional ping-pong between emails, texts, social media posts, and other distractions. With instantaneous access to information nearly everywhere you turn, it's no wonder we get sidetracked. Do you find yourself constantly multitasking and succumbing to this trap? Or perhaps you're good at getting started but have a hard time following through on tasks? A key part of being mentally tough is knowing where to direct your focus, how to maintain it and ignore distractions, and how to shift focus according to demands. There is no substitution for concentration and focus if you want to crush your goals and lead the life of your dreams!

Like the other components of mental toughness you've learned about, attentional focus is a muscle—it must be exercised to stay strong. So if you're someone who is constantly "connected" and continually distracted, you're in luck. The exercises in this chapter will train you to sharpen your attention both internally (controlling mental and emotional cues) and externally (controlling environmental cues). Now you can take your focus to the next level!

EXERCISE 109:
CREATE A DISTRACTIONS LIST

Did you know that once you get distracted it takes an average of twenty-five minutes to return to the previous focus of your original task? When you shift your energy back and forth between tasks, your attention gets drained.

How many times have you told yourself you were going to get something done but then found yourself inundated with internal distractions? You really want to stay focused, but for some reason you keep remembering things you need to pick up from the grocery store, emails you need to send, and topics you're just dying to learn more about. In order to sustain focus, you need to develop strategies to keep these distractions at bay.

TAKE IT TO THE NEXT LEVEL

While you're trying to focus and get some meaningful work done, keep your notebook next to you. Whenever a distracting thought pops into your head, simply jot it down and then refocus your attention on your work. This will signal to your brain that the thought has been acknowledged and will be addressed at a later time, allowing you to keep your attentional focus on the task at hand.

When you've finished your work, review this distractions list and make a plan for taking care of those items. This may include adding them to a to-do list, setting reminders on your phone, or getting them done right now.

EXERCISE 110:
SHARPEN YOUR MEMORY

Your working memory capacity plays a key factor in your ability to focus, resist distractions, and solve problems. Remembering a phone number or directions when you don't have a pen or smartphone handy, or incorporating the information you just researched into a term paper, are all examples of working memory. It's kind of like a blackboard in your brain where you keep relevant information while you're using it.

But the blackboard is only so big! New thoughts and experiences are constantly trying to erase your focused thoughts and make their way onto the board. However, that information will be easier to retain if you can reinforce what you've learned at regular intervals—for example, repeating that phone number or those directions every couple of minutes, just when you're about to forget.

TAKE IT TO THE NEXT LEVEL

Follow these steps to strengthen your working memory:

1. Memorize four details about someone you encounter early in your day. For example, your friend was wearing a black T-shirt, jean shorts, white sunglasses, and red lipstick.
2. Every couple of hours throughout the day, recall those details before you forget them. Extra points if you can wake up the next morning and remember all four details.

Do this exercise often, and once you've gotten good at it, increase either the number of details or the number of people (or both!) that you will try to memorize.

EXERCISE 111:
TRY TIME BLOCKING

Do you think you handle competing tasks with ease and efficiency? Studies show that only about 2.5 percent of people are able to multitask effectively! The majority are just creating possibilities for more mistakes to be made and stresses to run high.

If you're one to partake in multitasking madness, it's probably because it's hard to drown out all the distractions in your life. Picture this: You need to get a big project done because the deadline is approaching, but another task also seems important—and so does this one—and now your phone is ringing and you need to answer an email. In this scenario, both demands from other people and other tasks are acting as distractions from what you really need to be doing: working on the big project.

Time blocking can help you regain control of your attention, especially when you're faced with long or complex tasks. Instead of shifting your attention from one thing to the next, you fully devote your attention to one task for a specific block of time—no distractions, no exceptions! Once done, you reward yourself with a quick break, and then you do it again. Over time, this technique will condition you to focus exclusively on whatever task is at hand while increasing your discipline and productivity. Before you know it, your mental strength will reach new heights!

TAKE IT TO THE NEXT LEVEL

Follow these steps for time blocking when you need to tackle a complex task or project, or one that will take you at least twenty-five minutes to complete:

1. Decide on the task you want to focus on.
2. Get yourself in a distraction-free zone. That may mean putting your phone on airplane mode, disabling notifications on your laptop, and logging out of social media. Let people know that you're unavailable.
3. Make sure you have a glass of water and anything else you might need on hand for the next twenty-five minutes or more.
4. Set a timer for twenty-five minutes and start working on only that task. This is focused, uninterrupted work. If you succumb to a distraction at twenty-two minutes, you must reset the timer and start again.
5. When the timer is up, reward your hard work with a five-minute break. Give yourself a stretch, use the restroom, grab some fresh air, send a quick text—do whatever you have to do to prepare for the next block of uninterrupted time.
6. Set the timer again for twenty-five minutes and get to work. When the timer goes off, you get another five-minute break.

Repeat this process several times until you feel the need for a longer break. A good rule of thumb is to aim for four time blocks and then give yourself a longer break of twenty minutes or so. Once you've gotten the hang of it, try working with longer time blocks of thirty, forty, or even sixty minutes. See what works best for you.

EXERCISE 112:
KNOW YOUR LIMITS

These days, it's possible to find just about anything you're looking for on the Internet. Want to learn how to knit? There are thousands of *YouTube* videos that can teach you how. Want to learn more about the different parts of the brain and how they affect thought and emotion? There are countless online articles waiting for you. Or maybe you need a pick-me-up, so you head over to *Facebook*, because you know your quirky aunt has posted at least five ridiculous videos today. Or you turn to *Instagram* for guaranteed photos of your friend's new puppy. Now you need to get informed, so you hop on *Twitter* to get caught up on the latest political scandal.

You get the picture. This is the age of twenty-four-seven connectivity. It's easy to get carried away and lose hours of precious time that could be used to accomplish the things you actually want to accomplish. To avoid getting sidetracked by the Internet, mentally tough people set limits for themselves.

TAKE IT TO THE NEXT LEVEL

Whenever you use your smartphone or computer for something that isn't the task you should be focusing on, set a predetermined limit for it. What is a reasonable time or progress limit for each of these distractions? For example, you can only scroll through *Instagram* for ten minutes at a time (time limit), or you must stop watching *YouTube* after three videos (progress limit).

Use your best judgment when making these rules, and customize them to suit you. If you know you get more distracted by a string of three-minute teaser videos than one longer TED

Talk, create separate limits for both. If you take only one break to use social media per day, maybe your limits are a little longer, restricted to the morning or evening. If you know you're going to take three or four breaks throughout the day, keep your limits shorter and spread them out. To keep track of your main distractions and the limits you set for them—especially when first trying this exercise—keep a list in your notebook.

Your list might look something like this:

DISTRACTION	TIME OF DAY/ DAY OF WEEK	TIME OR PROGRESS LIMIT
Instagram	During work hours	Not allowed
	In the evening	Once, for 30 minutes
	On the weekend	No limit
Short YouTube videos (less than 5 minutes)	During work hours	One per break
	In the evening	Up to five videos
	On the weekend	No limit
Long YouTube videos (more than 5 minutes)	During work hours	Not allowed
	In the evening	Up to three videos
	On the weekend	No limit

Take any notes on how a limit does or doesn't work for you so you can adjust as necessary. After a few days, you may not need to refer to your list anymore.

EXERCISE 113:
DEVELOP A TRIGGER WORD

A trigger word is any word that evokes strong emotions in the listener. You see and hear these kinds of words everywhere, from websites and email newsletters to pop-up ads and the nightly news. Marketers and media use them to get you to click, read, and purchase.

What's this got to do with attentional focus? These powerful words can be used for more than just boosting sales and engagement. Everyone from athletes to business professionals use them covertly to improve their concentration and performance during high-pressure situations. To deal with nerves and refocus their energy, an athlete might use the word *focus*, *confidence*, or *calm*—either said silently in their head or quietly out loud—just before a big game. An employee about to make a big presentation might use more specific reminders, like *posture*, *projection*, or *concise*. Even a family member facing a difficult conversation can use trigger words to keep their cool and focus on communicating their message clearly and lovingly. When you devote your attention solely to the trigger word and the powerful meaning behind it, it's nearly impossible to think about anything that might be attempting to distract or unnerve you.

The possibilities are endless; just be sure your trigger word or phrase is short, powerful, and positively phrased.

TAKE IT TO THE NEXT LEVEL
Follow these steps to develop your own unique trigger word:

1. Consider what area of your life you could use a trigger word to hone your performance focus.
2. Determine your trigger word or phrase. Remember, you want to be able to recall the word quickly and have it immediately pull you into focus; it should be short, powerful, and intuitive.
3. Optional: Write the word(s) down in a prominent place as a visual reminder—perhaps on the palm of your hand or a sticky note that you can place on your laptop, notebook, or desk.
4. Intentionally practice using your word before "game day" (or presentation day or whatever!) in order to etch the word and its powerful meaning in your mind.
5. Use your trigger word to maximize your success.

EXERCISE 114: LISTEN ACTIVELY

Have you ever been engaged in conversation with someone and felt like they weren't really listening? Either their eyes were vacant—like they were thinking about something else—or you could tell they were just waiting for the moment you stopped talking so that they could jump in and say something. On the flip side, you've probably been engaged in conversation where the person was looking straight into your eyes, seemingly captivated by what you had to say. You likely felt heard and valued. That person was actively listening to you.

The big difference between passive and active listening is that with the latter, you listen with all your senses and give your full attention to whoever is speaking. You don't try to fill moments of silence or provide opinions or judgments—you are simply acting as a sounding board for them. It will be your turn to talk later! Fully immersed in the conversation, you may also reflect back pieces of what was said and offer nonverbal feedback (like nodding or leaning in) to show signs of active listening.

When you listen, are you hearing the complete message that's being communicated to you? If you want to establish better relationships and earn the trust of others, this is an amazing skill to master. And because it also requires complete focus and concentration on the person speaking, it's an excellent tool for honing your attentional focus overall.

TAKE IT TO THE NEXT LEVEL

For this exercise, take what you've learned (or already knew) about active listening and put it to use in your next conversation.

- Give them your complete and utter attention
- Use nonverbal cues to indicate that you're listening
- Reflect back what was said ("Okay, so what you're saying is...")
- Ask questions for clarification
- Be open, neutral, and patient

To take this exercise one step further, start practicing active listening every time it makes sense. The more experiences you have, the stronger your listening skills will become!

EXERCISE 115: DO DEEP WORK

Due to an increasingly digitalized world, many believe that attention spans are shrinking as people find it more and more difficult to filter out irrelevant stimuli. To develop mental toughness, you need to routinely practice the art of attentional control so that you can focus on what needs to be done in even the hardest circumstances.

There are four types of attention. Sustained and selective attention is required for deep, focused work—the kind of attention you need to pursue ambitious and meaningful goals. These days, most people are working from a place of divided or alternating attention—both of which actually weaken cognitive ability and are not nearly as good at tuning out distractions.

Because it's unlikely that you'll be able to sustain your attention for the entire day, how can you hone your focus when it really matters, and work smarter on your most important tasks? By concentrating on deep work over shallow work. Coined by author Cal Newport, *deep work* is defined as "professional activities performed in a state of distraction-free concentration that push your cognitive capabilities to their limit." Deep work creates value and improves your skills. On the other hand, "shallow work" is defined as "noncognitively demanding, logistical-style tasks, often performed while distracted." Shallow work typically doesn't create value. To level up your mental toughness and achieve success, you'll need to determine when you should be doing deep work and set yourself up for success.

TAKE IT TO THE NEXT LEVEL

Take a look at your average week. Make a list of all the tasks you generally perform, then circle anything that you consider deep work (during which you need uninterrupted, deep concentration and focus for a long period of time).

Now create a strategy for anytime you're going to sit down and do deep work. Remember, this is a distraction-free zone! Here are some tips to get you started:

- Stop multi-screening (using multiple devices at once)
- Turn off your smartphone or phone notifications, or put your devices on airplane mode
- Try time blocking (see the "Try Time Blocking" exercise in this chapter)
- Stay off social media
- Take technology-free, restorative breaks, such as a quick walk or meditation
- Consider using software (e.g., Freedom, RescueTime, and Mindful Browsing) that either blocks or limits the amount of time you can spend on distracting websites and apps

The more you practice doing deep, concentrated work, the more improvements you will see in your ability to stay focused.

EXERCISE 116: MEDITATE

You may have noticed that the concept of mindfulness has come up a number of times in your journey to level up. This is because mindfulness is centered on the ability to be aware and to calmly respond, rather than react, to your environment—key components of mental toughness.

The terms *mindfulness* and *meditation* are often used interchangeably, which can be confusing. Mindfulness is a way of living; it means being able to step back from racing thoughts and feelings to focus wholly on the present moment. Meditation, on the other hand, is like the training ground for learning mindfulness. It's a simple way to calm a busy, distracted mind so you can practice being in the present. There's also a common misconception that meditation is about making your mind go blank. Well, unless you're a Buddhist monk, that's probably next to impossible! Thoughts are always going to pop up. Meditation is a way to access the quiet that's buried underneath those thoughts—not silence them. Moving beyond your mind's chatter to that deeper quiet will help you develop a clear and focused mind, even long after you're done meditating.

TAKE IT TO THE NEXT LEVEL

The following are simple instructions for learning how to meditate. For one week, add meditation to your morning or evening routine. Or maybe you meditate on your lunch break or in between projects. Pick anytime that feels right for you, when you know you won't be interrupted.

As for how long you should meditate, that's completely up to you! You can start small—say, five minutes at a time—and work your way up to longer—maybe ten, fifteen, or twenty minutes. Use a timer and try to stay with it until the timer goes off.

1. Set your timer.
2. Find a comfortable seated position and close your eyes and mouth.
3. Focus all your attention and awareness on the feeling of your breath as you breathe through your nose. Pick any spot to focus on—either the air coming in and out of your nose, or the rise and fall of your chest or belly.
4. As soon as you notice that you are thinking about something, bring your attention back to your breath. This will happen over and over, and each time, just bring your focus back to your breath.

Meditation is the ultimate exercise in honing your attentional focus. Train your brain through meditation any time of day, as many times as you like. Or use it to achieve a more focused mind on the spot.

EXERCISE 117: DETERMINE YOUR OPTIMAL TIME

Do you consider yourself a morning person or a night owl? While that awareness is a good start, applying a more systematic approach can help you optimize your days for focus.

Your brain works differently as the day progresses, and science proves there are best and worst times to tackle certain types of work. However, everyone is a little bit different. Age, sex, and social and environmental factors all play a role in what times are best for you. To hone your attentional focus, get in sync with your own optimal times and work this insight into your routine.

You will want to get in the habit of doing your most important work during your peak productivity hours—essentially, tackling deep work (see the exercise "Do Deep Work" in this chapter) when your brain is the most focused. The lower your energy level, the harder it is for your brain to filter out distractions, so use the times when focus is most difficult for activities that need little to no attention.

TAKE IT TO THE NEXT LEVEL

For the next three weeks, track your levels of focus, energy, and motivation to find your sweet spot for productivity. You might begin to see some trends after just one week, but the longer you keep track, the more reliable your insights will be.

At the same times every day—try hourly intervals—record your focus/energy/motivation level and how much you're getting accomplished. Track how you feel. There may be times where you feel like you're on a roll. Write that down! Be as consistent as possible with your logging. Also take note of anything that may be affecting your scores for the day, such as lack of sleep or too much caffeine.

After the three weeks (or whenever you feel you have enough data), you should be able to see some patterns. Take note of when you were the most and least focused, when you noticed a surge or dip in your energy and motivation, or when you had to reach for a coffee. Once you've figured out your peak time(s) of day, see how you can optimize your time in order to take advantage of those insights. Save your most productive hours for projects or tasks that involve deep work, complex thought, and problem-solving. And as much as you're able to, try to protect your peak hours from other commitments or distractions that don't require your full brain power.

EXERCISE 118: READ WITH INTENTION

According to research, over a quarter of Americans didn't read a single book in 2018. And with so much engaging, relevant, visually appealing content available online, it's easy to see why people may be reading less. From blogs to podcasts to video posts, you can get informed instantaneously and move on to the next task on your to-do list.

However, this commitment to only bite-sized pieces of content is creating habits that impair your concentration and ability to remember important information. You're training your mind to only look for quick answers rather than explore complex concepts. Actively reading a book, on the other hand, can improve brain function, including attention span and memory. It's even believed that when the mind is fully focused on reading and nothing else, the body releases muscle tension and becomes deeply relaxed!

TAKE IT TO THE NEXT LEVEL

To complete this exercise you will simply need to read with intent. Whether you buy, borrow, or blow the dust off a book you've been meaning to read—it doesn't matter. The challenge is to dive deep into whichever book you choose, and focus completely on what you're reading.

If you can, take notes as you read (these can be done in the margins if you own the book, or in your notebook). Taking notes will train your attention and memory even further. Commit to reading for a minimum of five minutes each day and regain control of your mind.

EXERCISE 119: GET ORGANIZED

Remarkable productivity and focus don't just happen on their own! The most successful individuals prioritize organization, understanding that the best results come when you are able to find everything you need when you need it. The more disorganized your life is, the more likely you are to feel unfocused, unprepared, and overwhelmed.

It will be much easier to level up in all aspects of life if you have a process for staying organized and keeping clutter and distractions at bay. Once you start implementing a personal organization process and begin to see your productivity soar, there's a good chance you'll get hooked and never fall back on chaotic ways.

TAKE IT TO THE NEXT LEVEL

Grab your notebook and reflect on how you stay organized in your life—and how you don't. Where do you feel the most organized? Can you find the work documents you need when you need them—whether on your computer or in a physical filing system? Is your email inbox filtered according to your priorities? Where do you feel the most disorganized? Is there physical clutter that makes it impossible to focus? Is time management your Achilles' heel?

After exploring your current strategies for staying organized, use your spare time for an entire week to overhaul whichever processes are not working for you. Create a process for managing your inbox(es), for saving different passwords, for remembering dates and times, for keeping your clothes where they belong, for keeping track of content you want to read later...whatever will make you feel more calm and able to focus on what matters.

EXERCISE 120: VISUALIZE SUCCESS

A somewhat abstract concept in the realm of success and self-improvement is visualization. Because everything you do begins as a thought, the ability to visualize yourself doing it and achieving the outcome that you want is actually proven to increase your chances! Just as you would mentally rehearse what you're going to say or do during a presentation, interview, or even a date or sports game, visualization helps you prepare and get laser focused on the task you're about to perform. It is a mindfulness technique that adds vivid, highly detailed internal images to your mental rehearsal. Additionally, it helps combat nerves and increases your optimism about what lies ahead.

TAKE IT TO THE NEXT LEVEL

Start practicing visualization now so you can increase your ability to focus and be at the top of your game in any future endeavor. The performance you visualize can be anything from a conversation with your supervisor to a speech in front of a crowded auditorium to a soccer game—even your private attempt to beat your own best running time. As you follow these steps for visualization, keep in mind that the key to any effective mental practice is to be as specific as possible:

1. Find a quiet space where you won't be interrupted, and find your center (see the "Find Your Center" exercise in Chapter 7).
2. Set the scene for your performance. What does the space/venue look like? What is the lighting like? What are you wearing? Is there an audience? Will you be using any props? What is your body language like? Add other sensory input where applicable. Hear the chatter of the audience or the birds chirping. What does the temperature feel like?
3. Now visualize your positive performance from beginning to end. You are confident, prepared, focused, and calm. From walking into the space to looking around, introducing yourself (if applicable), and crushing your performance, walk through every step. Envision everything

going smoothly, but also be realistic. If you foresee a difficulty, visualize yourself overcoming it.

4. Envision what it will be like once your performance is successfully completed. If there's an audience, will they applaud? Or afterward tell you, "Great job"? Will you be awarded a medal? What will that process look like? Whatever success means to you, imagine what it will look and feel like.

INDEX

ABOUT THE AUTHOR

Michelle Ribeiro is a writer and certified life coach specializing in mental health. She holds an honors bachelor of commerce degree from McMaster University, along with a life coaching certification from the Centre for Applied Neuroscience—both in Ontario, Canada. She is also a registered yoga teacher with Yoga Alliance, and has instructed in various countries around the world. Her coaching practice calls on teachings from neuroscience, positive psychology, mindfulness, and yoga to support adults living with depression and/or attention-deficit/hyperactivity disorder (ADHD). As a complement to medical treatment, mental health coaching is action-oriented, with an emphasis on systems and routines for managing difficult symptoms, obtaining and maintaining stability, and resilience training.

Having gone through her own journey with mental illness, Michelle's expertise is based on decades of personal experience as well as study. Her approach is holistic, addressing the mental, physical, emotional, and spiritual realms as vital parts of an integrative system. Deeply attuned to the needs of others, Michelle's calling is to facilitate the very process of self-healing and self-discovery that led her down her own path to recovery.

To get in touch with Michelle or to learn more about her offerings, visit her website at MentalHealthCoaching.ca. Her writing can be found on PositivePsychology.com. For further insightful and uplifting content, give her a follow on *Instagram* @mindful.way.